Dedication

For my wife Michele, daughter Piper and son Gavin. I am very grateful for your understanding when I am writing. I wish I were easier to get along with and I love you all very much.

Acknowledgements

Mom and Dad who let me make my own mistakes, East Cobb Writer's Circle, Iron Sharpening Iron: Christian Speculative Fiction Authors, Secret Editor Man who has been around for a long time, my church pastors; Brian Germano and Jim Perry for their encouragement in my seeking the truth, to Paul Thomas I couldn't have done it without you sir, and for everyone else who encouraged my writing, thanks for not squashing the dream.

Chapter 1

You Are Well-Made

You are a well-made person. You don't really need someone else to say that, but I'll say it anyway; you are a well-made person. Before we get any further you need to accept this fact. No one else knows how your life has gone to this point but you. No one else knows the things that have been present to drive your choices, the reasons behind those choices, or what you have had to go through. It is unfair to make judgments based only on the cover of the book without opening up the cover and reading the pages. You are a well-made person. You feel a pull to something greater than yourself calling you to be a part of it; to contribute through your unique talents and gifts, but you aren't sure what it is or where.

> [31] God saw all that He had made, and behold, it was very good. And there was evening and there was morning, the sixth day.
> **Genesis 1:31 (NASB)**
>
> [16] "For God so loved the world, that He gave His only begotten Son, that whoever believes in Him shall not perish, but have eternal life.
> **John 3:16 (NASB)**

You were created and pronounced good just like all other things on the face of the earth. I know this is true because God said so in His word at Genesis 1:31. This is the passage where God finished creating everything, stood back and surveyed everything, and pronounced all of it 'Good'. That includes your creation as well. You are well-made from the mouth of the Supreme Being. What that does not pronounce as good are necessarily all the human choices you or I make over the course of our lives, but it does say the person, in general, is of good construction.

Another way I know you are well-made is that God sacrificed His only son for *all* the world, not just some people in the world. It says so in John 3:16. All means you, too. If God believes you are well-made to the point of sending his only Son to die for you, then who am I to argue with that?

So, you are a good person. Even if you don't believe that I do. I think you are a good person. I think you are worth knowing. I think you have value to yourself and the world you may not even be aware of yet....if only you will give that goodness a chance to manifest itself. This doesn't take a lot of work. In fact, it will take no more work than continuing to read. You don't even need to let anyone know you are reading this, but if you want to make that goodness that God put inside you grow and flourish you have to at least keep reading. Just print a copy, and bury it under the extra towels in the bathroom. Read it during that special time you are trapped each day counting the repeating pattern on the wallpaper in the bathroom...again. It'll be a nice change.

You have heard Christians tell people they are going to Hell if they don't listen to them. I'm not like those Christians. I'm not going to tell you the way you live your life is going to send you to Hell. I don't care what lifestyle you are currently living, that statement stands. I am not going to tell you the things you have done in the past are going to send you to Hell, because I am not that kind of Christian. I am going to tell you that you are a good person. God loves you. He is waiting for you with arms outstretched, and He wants to take you into His kingdom. It is His choice who is worthy, not mine or anyone else's on this planet.

God Really is Waiting for You

This is not the imperfect vision of an earthly father; this is the vision of the One who is the perfect Father. Why is it we humans ascribe such earthly fallibility to God such as not seeing who we are inside? Inside of you is a good person and God knows that. God can see you at the core of your being, at your heart; and He knows you are struggling with your life, your choices, and who you are. He wants to help with those things. He knows you, and He knows how to help. I'm not going to read you the entire parable of the prodigal son from Luke chapter 15. I am going to point you to verse 20 of that chapter to say that this parable is, among other things, about how

> [20] So he got up and came to his father. But while he was still a long way off, his father saw him and felt compassion *for him*, and ran and embraced him and kissed him.
> **Luke 15:20 (NASB)**

6

God is going to act when any of His children return to Him, including you.

Returning to God is an easy thing to do. He is waiting like the father of the prodigal son. He wants to throw a party in your honor. He is waiting patiently, expectantly by the door of His house watching the horizon for you, because He misses your company. He created you uniquely in all of creation for a purpose. His purpose is lacking without your unique contribution. Just decide right now to read through all of this even when it starts to get uncomfortable or hard. Make that commitment to Him right now. It's easy to do. Just talk to Him in your head and He will listen. I guarantee it.

At this point you may be thinking about some offense or other you think you committed for which God cannot forgive you. Remember this is the One who created everything; forgiveness is easy for Him. Reread Genesis 1 and 2 if you want to reaffirm how able, capable, and powerful He is. God is not looking to punish

> [8] The one who does not love does not know God, for God is love.
> **1 John 4:8 (NASB)**

His children for the wrong things they have done, that's not how He works. If you want to see the base, true nature of God, find 1John 4:8 and read what God's word says about who He is and how we as His children can start to know Him.

God is the best kind of love though, unconditional love. He loves you no matter what you have done, who you are right now, or what you will do in the future. See, the best part about God's love is that if you honor Him with your continued presence and conversation, He will honor you by continuing to love you no matter what. God's love doesn't care if you mess up in the future because He knows your heart. He knows how human beings struggle with making good choices. He knows we have the best of intentions sometimes but fail to carry through on what we want to do. Even some of the greatest authors of the Bible struggled with this.

Paul, arguably one of the greatest New Testament writers struggled with his choices, too. This man went from the absolute best person at hunting down and executing Christians for their beliefs to one of the greatest workmen God has ever produced. Paul killed more Christians before he found God than anyone else in his time. He found God on the road to Damascus one day and turned everything around. He struggled with his choices too. In his own words in Romans 7:15. Paul explains how he not only struggles with his choices but fails to make good ones. God loved Paul for his continued efforts to help others and to get better at just being Paul. God loved him so much that much of the New Testament came from Paul's quill. If God can love one of the worst persecutors and murderers of Christians like Paul, He can love you too. Do not worry about your struggles in the future, just invite God to help along the way and He will walk with you the entire time.

You expected this to be a condemning conversation, and it isn't going to be. I'm not going to point the finger at you wagging it like a displeased parent telling you how disappointing you are. That isn't my task. I don't know you. I don't know what you've gone through, and you haven't invited me in to help. So, it is not my place to tell you what I think about how you live.

> [15] For what I am doing, I do not understand; for I am not practicing what I *would* like to *do*, but I am doing the very thing I hate.
> **Romans 7:15 (NASB)**
>
> [15] Call upon Me in the day of trouble; I shall rescue you, and you will honor Me.
> **Psalm 50:15 (NASB)**

You and God can take a private look at your life to figure out what changes He wants you to make for His purpose, not mine. I'm a fallible human being just like you. I make enough mistakes trying to direct my own life; I don't need to add making mistakes in your life, too. Talk with God. Let Him in and let Him decide what to change and when to change it.

God really is waiting for you to return right now. He even has a promise for you found in Psalm 50:15. Be forewarned though. If you call upon Him and He does help, you have to help back. Right now, your help comes in the form of just saying thank you and continuing to talk to Him. It's not complicated, but it is something He desperately wants; a continued conversation with you. Yes, He is God, and if He really wanted something, He could just take it; but that totally invalidates the greatest gift ever given; your free will. God is not in the business of breaking His own rules. He gave you the same ability to choose that He gave to Adam and Eve. He didn't take that away from them, and He won't take it away from you either. Ask Him to help and He will. Just keep talking to Him.

Because it is His decision to Take You Back if He Chooses to do so

In the human world we strive to wear the right clothes, to say the right things, to look a certain way; to fit in. Some head the opposite way and seek to separate themselves through those same methods; to stand out as special rather than be part of the herd. In God's eyes we are all special, because He knows exactly what went into creating us each the way we are, and He made us the way we are on purpose for a reason, His reason. That doesn't absolve us of the consequences of the choices we have made, it means we have a purpose, use, and value just as we are right now because God is wise enough and loving enough to know exactly how to best employ each of us. You were well-made, you have value, and God seeks to show you where you have the most value if you will ask Him to show you. He can use you, because He made all of this and the choice is His who He will use and for what. That choice does not rest with any human being no matter what others may tell you. It is a choice for God alone.

Since it's God's decision who gets into Heaven and who doesn't, have your conversation ready to allow others to share your journey, then open up and invite them in. God knows your heart. He knows what you are able to bear and not bear. He is walking with you along this road for both the uphill struggles and the downhill good times. Share this journey with Him and He will help carry your burdens because He wants to do so. You can be sure He is making a good decision with you because He can be trusted to be faithful to His ways, read Deuteronomy 32:4. Keep in mind this verse is about the nature of God, not the fallible human beings who are His followers. We make mistakes. We make bad decisions. We can

> [4] The Rock! His work is perfect, For all His ways are just; A God of faithfulness and without injustice, Righteous and upright is He.
> **Deuteronomy 32:4 (NASB)**

condemn or judge those whom He has found worthy, so for now keep the discussion in your head with Him. He can be trusted to guide you well when you are first starting out but know in your heart now that there will come a day when He will call you to share this journey with others. He will strengthen you for this time and not set it upon you until you are ready, but it is something He calls for when you have more experience with Him.

The authority to decide who gets into heaven or not is God's because He made it all. If you want to have some fun, read the book of Job. It is long and a little repetitive, but that is to make a point. The fun part comes at the end in chapters 38 and 39. If you don't want to read all of that focus on Job 38:4-6 but when you read this put a note of sarcasm in the voice of God as He asks these rhetorical questions of Job. Job has been railing against God for perceived slights. I envision God being tired of the complaining and finally deciding in exasperation to address His child. I'm not sure if God gets exasperated with us or not, but that is always how I have pictured this exchange. It is entertaining to envision God using sarcasm in Old Testament times to me though.

> [4] "Where were you when I laid the foundation of the earth? Tell *Me*, if you have understanding,[5] Who set its measurements? Since you know. Or who stretched the line on it?
> [6] "On what were its bases sunk? Or who laid its cornerstone,
> **Job 38:4-6 (NASB)**

This passage leads into the old joke about the modern scientists who thought they were as good as God since they could create things too, so God said to them, "Okay, let's see you do it" The scientists gather up some clay and form a person, then bring it to life and stand back admiring what they created. They turn to God to see his reaction and He says, "That's very good. Now create your own clay and do it again."

God derives His authority to decide who He will accept and not accept from the fact that He created everything from nothing. This grants Him sole authority over it all, not human beings who have read some of what is in His book and think they know everything (me included). We are fallible human beings. Walk with the one who is infallible to see what He says about you. He really is waiting to take you into His arms and hug on your neck, throw a party, and welcome you back; but you have to agree to this first by just talking with Him.

Starting the conversation is simple to do and there are several ways to do it. You can just have a conversation in your head with Him. He will hear and knows it is you. You could invite Him in through His Holy Spirit by reading His word in the Bible. We couldn't always do this, but it is a freedom we currently enjoy. If you are truly bold, you could approach a trusted friend who already has a relationship with God and ask him or her to help you. Or, you could begin a journal and write your conversations either on a computer or through old fashioned pen and paper. Whatever method you choose to use is up to you, either one of these or a different one all your own. Just have a conversation with Him. You will be amazed at the reaction both inside and out. But for now, it is okay to keep it all to yourself if you want.

Chapter 2

You Don't Need the Church to Read the Bible

Senior Pastors, Bishops, and Deacons around the world just fainted or stopped reading; but you don't need those people to read the Bible. You don't need anyone to read God's word. You've already bought into the idea (or already knew) that you are a well-made thing in the world because God made everything and pronounced it Good. That was Genesis 1:31 we read in the last chapter. You feel a pull to something greater than you and have decided it might be God so you've opened up and are having that conversation now, but you would like to deepen that conversation beyond the superficial small talk you've been having.

Many modern churches who want you to think spirituality cannot be done without them. I will grant them the truth that a maturing Christian does need the church. However, you do not need a church to read the Bible, and right now all you are looking to do is deepen the personal conversation you have been having with God and His son. Reading God's word about life in the Bible is the logical next step, and you can take that step on your own quite easily.

What the people in modern organized religion fail to see is how hypocritical some churches appear from the outside. Sometimes churches are their own worst enemies, but the problem isn't wholly from within the church. Those outside need to remember that all of Christianity isn't represented by the vision the modern mainstream media tends to portray. The organization that calls itself a church and protests dead soldier's funerals are not representative of Christianity (in fact they are a church in name only but that is not the focus of this writing.) The point here is that for every church you read about that is hypocritical there really are 100 churches out there who are walking in God's plan just as you are. They just wait to be discovered.

What we need now is a new definition of "Church". The old definition is viewed by those not in church as a gathering place for those holier-than-thou people who have a judgmental view of other people. This is what drove many, and possibly you too, away from the church. You know you are trying to be a good person, but others perhaps cannot see beyond the outward appearance or beyond past errors to see the change in you today. You still feel the love of God, which is that strange pull and attraction that has you seeking something more. You know you are needed but each time you have tried to find somewhere to "fit in" it just hasn't fit.

You've gotten the conversation with God going now but just the two of you. Maybe it's in your head when you feel like talking, or you have heard His voice speaking to you when you are out and about. Open that conversation to another member of His world, the Holy Spirit. This is how the next stage of a deepening personal relationship with God is formed. You are going to need a Bible to really hear the Holy Spirit, and we will talk about getting that in a minute. For now, realize that you can read the Bible with just you, God, and the Holy Spirit (which is really God too but we'll get into that more later). This is the next step in deepening the conversation with God.

The Holy Spirit's role in this relationship is a very important one. In simple terms, the Holy Spirit will help you hear the message God has for you better. Yes, God can communicate His own messages, but He has assigned this task and role to the Holy Spirit just as He assigned Judgment to Jesus. As you deepen the conversation through reading His word, insight into your life is opened up through the words in the Bible by the Holy Spirit so that you can take exactly the point you need right now. The Holy Spirit helps make connections between your understanding of the world and God's message so you can begin to build the structure of God's purpose in your life. We laid the foundation in the last chapter; and now, through your reading the Bible by yourself, you are beginning to build upon that foundation. You don't need a building full of people to take this next step. What you do need to realize is that the old definition of 'Church' is what we need as our new definition of church.

In those first years of the church they didn't have the Bible. They had personal letters from the Apostles who were there walking and talking with Jesus. Or, they had copies of the

Jewish scripture which Christians call the Old Testament. The letters the Apostles sent around plus recounts of Jesus' life, death, crucifixion, and resurrection are what make up the New Testament. These writings later became bound in a single tome. Today we call that book the Bible. The old definition of church from the first days of Peter until now was heavily rooted in God's word as contained in His Bible, rather than the words of man. Our new definition of church needs to look like our old definition of church, and that is attaching everything to His word.

In the time of Jesus, church was a small group of believers gathered at someone's house. They read the scripture and discussed its meaning. Jesus said it best in Matthew 18:20 that where two or three are gathered in His name, there He is also. That is important because Jesus is really the key to all this learning; He is why we want to read God's word, grow closer to God, and work at God's purpose in our lives.

> [20] For where two or three have gathered together in My name, I am there in their midst.
> **Matthew 18:20 (NASB)**
>
> [1] In the beginning was the Word, and the Word was with God, and the Word was God.
> **John 1:1 (NASB)**

Getting back to the old-school definition of church means rooting everything in God's word. What is God's word? John 1:1 tells us exactly what God's word is. Go read that scripture now. The Word as related here is a euphemism for Jesus, the Christ (Christ is a title, not a name meaning Anointed in Greek and is a translation of the Hebrew word for Messiah). Jesus completes the three pieces you need to deepen the conversation you've been having. God is the Father in heaven who presided over the creation of all things. The Holy Spirit is God making connections between His creation and His plans for each of us. Jesus is God who took on the form of a person to show us how He intended us to live according to His ways.

There is something you must understand about we human beings, and it is important to know before moving on. This truth doesn't change that you are well-made and were created good. It is merely a stone that needs to be placed on the foundation you have laid of God's word as contained in the bible. This stone goes next to the cornerstone we just laid by identifying Jesus as God Himself.

Man (men and women both are what we mean when we say "Man" with a capital M) is a fallen creation. This means that from a biblical sense we human beings have tendencies to do things God doesn't like. The Bible refers to these tendencies as "evil" or "sinful". This fact is captured by Paul in a portion of his letter to the Romans (read Romans 3:10). Note

> [10] as it is written," There is none righteous, not even one;
> **Romans 3:10 (NASB)**

Paul says "…not even one;" he is referring to who is doing things the way God likes, "…not even one." Many churches today like to point fingers at individuals and call them sinful laying blame for things squarely at their feet. That is not my method, but you have to understand that while I have been emphasizing that you are good, which I still believe; you must also realize all human beings have a tendency to do things God doesn't like.

We go back to Adam and Eve from the very beginning. They messed up and took bad advice from the serpent (who was the first appearance of Satan in the Bible). If you want to read the full story read Genesis 3 as a complete chapter. Verse 4 is the serpent giving bad advice, verse 6 is where men and women made the first bad choice, and verse 16 starts the punishment we received from God as a consequence of that bad choice.

Yes, God pronounced all of creation including Mankind, bad choices and all, as good. This tells us we are greater than the sum of those choices if we choose to be (yet another choice). We demonstrate that we've made that choice by talking with God and reading His word. You have made that choice, but the fact that you sometimes make bad choices cannot be displaced. Don't feel bad because all humans make bad choices from time to time, not just you (yes even those Christians who point fingers make bad choices including pointing that finger, in my view). This is not to excuse those bad choices, but to come to terms with it so we can get beyond it. God loves us even though from time to time we don't do what He wants us to do. The best part is He loves us all from that finger-pointing Christian to the worst person walking the planet right now. God loves us all, and He wants us to talk with Him about how we can do better.

God really does love us all, and He enjoys the conversations He has with us; He just wishes they would be more frequent. You find you spend more time talking with Him, but you feel that pull to something greater. Opening up the circle from just God to include His Holy Spirit and His Son Jesus is the next logical step through reading the Bible. Christians have been pointing fingers and telling you what God says in that book for a long time. It's time to find out for yourself what He says you should do instead of being told by those other people who make bad choices too.

What is the Bible and Why do You Need it?

We said the Bible is a collection of the Jewish scripture called the Old Testament and the writings of the early church Apostles called the New Testament bound together into one book (the word "Bible" comes from the Greek word *biblos* which means book). Each "Book" of the Bible was actually a single, bound book of loose papers or scrolls back in the first millennia of the Christian church. That is what the physical makeup of the Bible is, but it isn't what it *is*.

There are as many opinions about what the Bible is as there are people. When this topic comes up an 800-pound elephant is in the room, and no one wants to look at it. This is because there are two basic camps concerning what the Bible "is".

The first camp considers the Bible the work of human beings. There are those in this camp who take the title Christian, and there are those who oppose Christianity in this camp. Whether you are for or against Christ is irrelevant to this point. People in this camp believe the writings contained in the Bible came strictly from the minds of human beings put on paper to communicate human ideas to accomplish human goals.

Christians in the first camp believe those human goals are to better organize and order the worship of God, Jesus, and the Holy Spirit. Some of these people refer to the Bible as "divinely inspired" meaning God provided the idea only but men and women provided the actual words. These Christians lend significance to the Bible but do not make it an inviolate part of their life. For them, the Bible can be picked through for those points they agree with and discarded on points they disagree with because people wrote it.

For people in the first camp who are opposed to Christianity they generally believe the Bible was written by human beings for the purpose of controlling, continuing, and oppressing various segments of the world. A small percentage will agree the Bible is a collection of good moral values to live by but remains just another book. For the totality of people in this camp the Bible carries no more weight than any other book ever written and, in some cases, less because of the perceived controlling nature behind it.

The second camp of beliefs about the Bible is those who believe the Bible is from God, written by Him through human beings just as we would hold a pen to write a letter, and is infallible in its direction concerning how to live. Some people in this camp take every word in the Bible to mean exactly what it says, taking the Bible literally. Another segment of this camp believes there are alliterations in the Bible such as parables that teach valuable lessons but do not mean exactly what the literal words say. In both cases people in the second camp ascribe authority to the words contained in the book and try to order their lives as best they can around what they learn from it.

By way of full disclosure, I fall into this second camp. I believe God held the men and women attributed with authorship of the Bible as a pen. The words in the text are His words for us each. Through His Holy Spirit we individually get a personal message from scripture each time we read it. This unique message can be provided to individuals from the same text because, well, He is God and can do things like that. From a scriptural standpoint (I know the debaters in the crowd will say you can't use the Bible to prove the Bible but that's why it's called Faith) I can present you two passages that lend authority to this book.

The first passage is John 1:14, read that now. The book of John is the gospel that starts out at creation and moves through the highlights of Jesus' life. This passage explains that Jesus is the transformed word of God made into a man. The practical meaning of this is that Jesus became the

> [14] And the Word became flesh, and dwelt among us, and we saw His glory, glory as of the only begotten from the Father, full of grace and truth.
> **John 1:14 (NASB)**

Old Testament laws to demonstrate how God wanted a human

being to live here on earth. This is what was meant by the explaining statement Jesus made himself in Matthew 5:17.

The second passage of authority on what the Bible is comes from 2 Timothy 3:16. This passage is from Paul to his friend Timothy explaining how Timothy should view the world and conduct his ministry. Timothy, at the time, was just starting out in his work, and Paul was providing counsel on how to move that ministry forward.

> [17] "Do not think that I came to abolish the Law or the Prophets; I did not come to abolish but to fulfill.
> **Matthew 5:17 (NASB)**
>
> [16] All Scripture is inspired by God and profitable for teaching, for reproof, for correction, for training in righteousness;
> **2 Timothy 3:16 (NASB)**

Based on both these passages, my reasoning and experience, and the traditions of the faith I ascribe to; I believe the New Testament is a record of Jesus' example of how to do what the Old Testament meant for us to do. Human beings failed to comprehend God's instructions correctly in the Old Testament, so He came down here and showed us how to do it right by way of example, which was documented in the New Testament. I believe God guided each and every word written such that He, not man, is the author of the full book. I also believe there are no contradictions in the Bible, only situations we do not fully understand yet due to our failures as human beings or the limitations of our learning. When something is found in the Bible that *appears* as a contradiction what we have is a new topic for further study to better understand how it fits into the reality of creation. Supposed contradictions are not an invalidation of the work as a whole, they are a validation that we are flawed in our understanding of the Divine.

I further believe that you and I can read the same exact scripture and get opposite meanings from it that send us in opposite directions, and both of us are still walking along the path God has laid out for both of us. This last part is possible because He sees the Big Picture, and we do not. This allows Him to have us working in what seems like opposed efforts but are in reality supporting the overall goodness of His works as a whole.

What is the Bible? The Bible is God's manual for life. Everything we do should be based on this book and not the words of Man. The Bible is the number one way God gives us direction and talks to us. It is His number one spiritual "Road Sign" to guide us in our daily walk with Him. The Bible is an answer book for all the questions of life as long as we study it enough with a right heart open to the leadings of God's Holy Spirit. This is the key. The Holy Spirit or Holy Ghost, depending on what you like to call Him, is the one who can lead us through the minefields of life. If you base your beliefs on what you find in your personal studies of His word you are laying a further solid course of stone setting a firm foundation for the structure of your life, and you will not go wrong or stray from His path for you.

What Translation of the Bible Should I Read?

The short answer is you should read the translation you like the best. Don't let any reason to dislike a particular translation keep you from the word of God. Find another translation you do like so you can continue the conversation. There are so many translations now there is bound to be one you can find that you like. But you hear so much about the King James Version of the Bible, what is that and why is it so controversial?

The King James Version of the Bible, or KJV, was commissioned by King James in 1611 as a new translation to be based on the Bishops Bible in use then as well as about eight other complete or mostly complete manuscripts of the Greek New Testament. The manuscripts used at the time were no older than the tenth century, which puts them around one thousand years after the times of Jesus. In textual criticism circles the closer a manuscript is to the original date of the events it is about the more "authority" or "authoritative" it is said to be. Authoritative in this context means accurate. While this rule usually holds true, there is a reason that I believe it does not in this case.

Back in the days of the early church (circa 300AD) and until Gutenberg invented the printing press in 1440 the only way you could make a copy of any written document, including books, was to do it by hand. This meant hours and hours of laborious work meticulously copying the original. One task set to some monks in some monasteries was to accurately copy the Holy Bible.

To copy the Bible the monks created a system to ensure accuracy. After all, they needed to make sure they did not alter what God had passed on. Their system utilized several monks reviewing each word as it was written from the original page to the new page. If one of the reviewers determined a mistake was made the entire page would be destroyed and they would have to start again.

Beginning a new page had certain requirements as well. The monks would carefully measure the needed area to copy the text and outline that exact same area on the new page. They would then carefully copy the letters in the same size, what we would call the pitch of the letters today. The new page had to look exactly like the old page as far as the letters of the text went or it was deemed an inaccurate copy and destroyed.

Why is all this important to the KJV Bible? Bibles copied in this fashion were written on paper that was not a very good quality in those days. It wore out quickly if used frequently. A church was the only place you could generally find a copy of the Bible because of the high cost to produce one so it got used every day by those who served at that church. When it started to wear out they began sending pieces of it to the monks to get it recopied. The manuscript they had would be used until it wore out and then destroyed with the new copy taking its place. Any copy deemed to have "errors", "additions", or "corrections" would be destroyed as unprofitable for teaching God's word. If it was accurate it would be used for teaching until it wore out.

We can trust the eight or so tenth-century manuscripts from which the King James Version of the Bible was translated because they were that old and because we know the monks were meticulous in their methods of copying. Further, we have now discovered over 24,000 passages of ancient scripture ranging from the time of just after Jesus to the tenth century and just over 99% of all those 24,000 examples of scripture found agree, or match, the manuscripts used for the King James Version of the Bible.

If these statements are true about the KJV Bible, then why are there so many translations? Have you ever read the KJV Bible? The "English" used in it is fairly archaic and difficult to understand by modern standards. What this means is when you read the KJV Bible many people also need to read the dictionary, so they know what words like "froward", "fornicate", "discernment", and the like actually mean. Look them up and I bet you'll be surprised to find the "archaic" definitions, which is what was meant in this translation of the Bible. We have so many translations for the simple reason that many people want a more readable Bible. However, if you can learn to read the King James Version of the Bible smoothly, you can read anything smoothly. Additionally, reading the KJV Bible slows down your reading so you can chew over the scripture for better understanding rather than speeding through it as though it were a fiction novel.

Another reason we have so many translations revolves around the discovery of two complete Greek New Testaments that differ from those used for the King James Version. Finding a "new" copy of the ancient Greek New Testament manuscripts is a big deal. Finding one that is complete from Matthew to Revelation is almost unheard of. When the complete manuscript you find is from the third century, only 300 years after the time of Jesus, by textual criticism rules that are usually to be considered the most accurate of all the others. I do not agree with this statement in this case, and we will talk about that shortly.

The first of the two manuscripts found is called Codex Sinaiticus because it was found in a monastery on Mount Sinai by a man named Tischendorf. The date for this manuscript is somewhere between 325 and 360 AD. This manuscript was found in the basement of the monastery as a monk was cleaning up and burning old papers. The manuscript has over 3000 differences from other New Testament manuscripts, most of which are names, but some are significant. There are at least four different versions of handwriting, or copiers, and about five "correctors" who made additions or changes after the original copying. It is because this manuscript has so many corrections and errors that I believe it was not used in the church because they believed it was not accurate. This is why it was not used, worn out, and destroyed as happened with so many accurate copies of that time. Since its discovery, Codex Sinaiticus has been digitized and placed on the web. You can see pictures of the text here http://www.codex-sinaiticus.net/en/.

The second manuscript is called Codex Vaticanus because the manuscript is housed by the Vatican. Like Codex Sinaiticus this manuscript had multiple copiers and correctors, though not as many as the previous manuscript. Like Sinaiticus, Vaticanus also has many errors and omissions. Many scholars believe it to be a "more accurate" version of the Bible, but the evidence in my view is against this because of the number of fragments found that still agree with the Textus Receptus, which is the compiled Greek New Testament manuscript behind the KJV. Vaticanus is also from around the same 4th century time frame as Sinaiticus. Vaticanus also was found on a shelf in the Vatican gathering dust. I believe it was "gathering dust" because it was known to have too many errors and also not worthy of being used to teach.

This information is important to have as you go about selecting a translation you wish to read. While I firmly believe God will get whatever message He has for you through no matter what version you read information is important any time you see a footnote in a Bible revolving around something like, "The oldest texts..." they are referring to these two manuscripts. Investigate these manuscripts for yourself but pay close attention to two examples when you do. The end of the Book of Mark is a prime example of what I term "egregious" errors in transmitting the word of God through these two manuscripts.

Mark 16:9-20 are omitted in both manuscripts, but the omission itself isn't what is interesting. It is the visual of each page where it is omitted that I find interesting here. In the Vaticanus manuscript the chapter of Mark ends at verse 8 with blank space after it. If you were to continue copying verses 9-20 in the same size text, they would exactly fit into the empty space left. In Codex Sinaiticus the letter size suddenly enlarges and fills out the remaining space. If those letters were reduced to the size of the other letters in Mark, you have just enough space to fit verses 9-20. Additionally, the last four pages were not the original pages written for the rest of the Book of Mark and were written by a later copyist for some unknown reason.

So, if God can get His message through to us via any translation He wants, why does it matter which translation you read? It doesn't matter to me. Just make sure it is a translation and not a paraphrase.

A paraphrase is a version of the Bible where the people writing it decide what a passage really means and then put it into different words to better convey the meaning. They are not telling you exactly what the Greek or Hebrew words were that were written and what the modern English equivalent is, they are trying to tell you what it *should mean*. This is dangerous ground because it can be colored by the background of the person writing the paraphrase.

Many people in society today do not want to read the Bible to hear what God thinks about what people do. There are passages in the Bible where God says some things are wrong. No one wants to hear they are doing something God doesn't like, but because we are fallen human beings who are not perfect, we make mistakes. We need a perfect example to show us how to do things and that is what Jesus gave us, and what is written in the Bible. Some translators have proceeded with the intent of altering God's word to fall more in line with what they thought it should say rather than what God said. Finding out which is which is for you to decide as you educate yourself and grow closer to God.

God is God. He can get His message to us through the phone book if He wanted to. Read the translation you like that is easiest for you to follow but do this with your heart open to the leadings of the Holy Spirit. This is how we ensure we get the message God has for us. Pray each time you read the Bible that the Holy Spirit will enter your heart and give you the message God has for you that day.

What Other Tools Are There to Grow In Understanding?

You are having a conversation with God. You are growing closer to Him and His word. You've even found a copy of the Bible you like and are reading it, but that pull to something greater is still there; the hunger to move forward is driving you to seek more information. Here are some tools to add to your new library that will expand the things for you to think about, study, and take in as you walk along this path with God.

The Greek/English Interlinear New Testament

This book is an invaluable resource. It is a large book that contains copies of the actual Greek words contained in the original manuscript used for the translation it was written about. You can get an interlinear New Testament to show you the Greek words behind any of the translations out there for the most part.

The interlinear book is set up in a specific way to aid you as you study. Usually the Greek text takes up the majority of the page and right under each word is the English word that most closely equals that Greek word. This is called the literal translation. In a column on one side of the page are usually the words that appear in the Bible based on the literal translation. This book is most useful to you when it is coupled with the next book, a Greek/English Bible dictionary, and those get better when a concordance is added to the mix.

The Greek/English Bible Dictionary

The Greek/English Bible dictionary is most useful because it usually uses Strong's Numbers to reference each word in a particular Bible translation to the Greek word behind it. This allows you to look up the meaning of the Greek word outside of the context it was used in to see how it might also be used in other contexts.

The wonderful thing about the Greek language of the New Testament is that Greek words generally didn't mean just one thing. They were much richer in meaning. Learning the other intended usages of a word adds rich flavor to reading God's word that English sometimes lacks.

The Bible Concordance

The biblical concordance for the translation you have chosen is a nearly indispensable tool for study. This book allows you to take a word like Hope, Faith, or Love and see all the passages in the Bible where that word appears. You can then study all those scriptures as a group to better understand what that word means when God uses it. This will allow you to ask your own questions of God and receive your own answers with enough diligent study. Concordances exist for all the translations of the Bible for the very purpose of aiding you in your growth with God.

Commentaries

While you are walking with God alone and studying on your own, Commentaries are ways to add a person to the discussion without actually adding another person. Commentaries are books where you can look up a specific passage of scripture and see what historically great theologians thought about that same passage. When doing this you should make sure you take into account who the person writing the commentary was as this may give you some insight into why that person thought the way they did and used the terms they used.

Commentaries give you a voice of counsel from great minds of the past who were highly revered in the church, but it is unfortunately only a one-way discussion.

Where Do You Go from Here?

This walk with God is beginning to grow. You are having a conversation with God based on His word because He thinks you are a well-made person and wants to be with you. He is interested in helping you grow into the purpose He has for you through this conversation in His word. Returning to the basics by founding everything you do on how He directs your life through His word is an excellent foundation, but a foundation is not the end of a building, it is the beginning of a structure.

If you want to get back to the single most basic element of Christian belief, we must go back to the beginning of time through the beginning of one of the best-loved Gospels, the Gospel of John. In John 1:1 he says speaking of God's word and His Son, "In the beginning was the Word, and the Word was with God, and the Word was God." If you want to know who 'The Word" was to John, you will have to keep reading. You will probably have it by the time you reach verse 14 where John drops a big hint, but by the end of the first chapter you will know who he is talking about.

Okay, I'll just tell you, The Word is Jesus. God took His Word, and made it flesh in the form of His Son, Jesus, who was the Christ. What this means is the things God spoke of all throughout the Old Testament were born in the form of a man. If we base our understanding of God through the New Testament teachings of Jesus, we can know God, know how God wants us to live, and know-how God wants us to live together. It is the most basic of Christian principles and all your learning should start here.

Where do you go from here? First you pray, which is just having conversations with God. Yes, talking to God is prayer. You don't need a seminary degree to pray. You don't need a diploma to pray, you don't even need to own a Bible to pray. You just need to want to talk to God, and it is prayer. So, pray. Pray that God will teach you what He wants you to know. Pray that

[1]The Lord is my shepherd, I shall not want. [2] He makes me lie down in green pastures; he leads me beside quiet waters. [3]He restores my soul; He guides me in the paths of righteousness for His name's sake. [4]Even though I walk through the valley of the shadow of death, I fear no evil, for you are with me; your rod and your staff, they comfort me. [5]You prepare a table before me in the presence of my enemies; you have anointed my head with oil; my cup overflows. [6]Surely goodness and loving kindness will follow me all the days of my life, and I will dwell in the house of the Lord forever.

Psalm 23 (NASB)

[7] "And when you are praying, do not use meaningless repetition as the Gentiles do, for they suppose that they will be heard for their many words. [8] So do not be like them; for your Father knows what you need before you ask Him. [9] "Pray, then, in this way: 'Our Father who is in heaven, Hallowed be Your name. [10] ' Your kingdom come. Your will be done, On earth as it is in heaven. [11] ' Give us this day our daily bread. [12] 'And forgive us our debts, as we also have forgiven our debtors. [13] 'And do not lead us into temptation, but deliver us from] evil. For Yours is the kingdom and the power and the glory forever. Amen.'

Matthew 6:7-13 (NASB)

God will give you the tools to prosper His way. Pray that God will lead you through the valley of the shadow of death so that you will fear no evil as it says in Psalm 23. Pray for these things and pray as Jesus taught us to pray in Matthew 6:7-13 so that the things you are forgetting to pray about are covered because God knows what you need better than you do.

What now? You will have questions all the commentaries cannot answer. Things will come up which the Holy Spirit will show you that must by definition involve another human being, if you are to learn what God intends for you to learn. When you are ready, and with the Holy Spirit in your heart, you will have to move outside yourself and find a church, because if you are to continue your growth to become the person God truly intends you to be, you will have to involve other people.

Why do you need a church? When you are ready you will not just need one but want one. You will want to have holy conference with other committed students of God's word like yourself. You will crave that connection just as you currently feel that pull to something greater that has lead you to God, Himself. Being with God and learning about Him eventually means that you will have to learn about others, too. God didn't send His Son to sacrifice Himself for you alone, but for all the world as we have seen in

John 3:16. God loves everyone just as much as He loves you. You have many wonderful gifts God intends for you to put to use to make other lives better, not just your own.

This is a scary concept, but it is one we can tackle together. Just as God won't leave you alone out there, neither will I. You can find a church that is right for you where they will treat you as you know God would intend, with loving-kindness. This walk will not be always covered in roses and flower petals because there are other fallen human beings on the path, but you have the Creator of all things at your side; and if God is with you then who can be against you (read Romans 8:31-32). This doesn't mean you get to have all the stuff you want, but it does mean you have the best ally every conceived through the Holy Spirit in Jesus Christ and God the Father. If you want to fully discover your purpose with God, you will have to begin to find a church, or you will never fully satisfy that pull you feel to something greater.

> [31] What then shall we say to these things? If God *is* for us, who *is* against us? [32] He who did not spare His own Son, but delivered Him over for us all, how will He not also with Him freely give us all things?
> **Romans 8:31-32 (NASB)**

Chapter 3

A Personal Commitment to God

I have been saying the love of God is for everyone, and it is. The people reading this who already have self-worth do not have an issue with this statement encompassing them. Those who read this statement and have a low self-image do not feel they are worthy of such love. There is something in this statement to learn for both classes of people.

If you have a low self-image you must understand the love of God is for you. If you wonder how anyone can love someone as broken as you feel you are, consider the following two things. First, read John 3:16. The love of God is for "...the world..." that "...whoever believes in Him..." This is not for a select few, it is for everyone, and that includes you. Second, we are talking about God here. If that first point is not enough, consider this. The One who decided how to create all matter in the universe decided you are worthy of His attention. There is nothing He cannot do (we use the masculine pronoun for God because it is traditional, but the Bible is quite clear that God is made of both male and female as one). Do not tell God there is something He cannot do.

For the second class of people who already have a solid self-image and have no issue believing God can love them, hear this. That same love God extends to you is extended for all people in all the world, even the ones you don't think deserve it.

There is a word in the Bible you need to understand, and that word is grace, read Ephesians 2:8-10.

> [16] "For God so loved the world, that He gave His only begotten Son, that whoever believes in Him shall not perish, but have eternal life.
> **John 3:16 (NASB)**
>
> [8] For by grace you have been saved through faith; and that not of yourselves, *it is* the gift of God; [9] not as a result of works, so that no one may boast. [10] For we are His workmanship, created in Christ Jesus for good works, which God prepared beforehand so that we would walk in them.
> **Ephesians 2:8-10 (NASB)**

Grace is a gift from God but not because we earned it. For now, it is enough to just know grace equals a gift. Later, you can dig more into the meaning of grace. However, from this passage take away that you receive this gift each time you renew your trust in God through faith that Jesus died for all the world to bring them back to God. God offers this gift to you without condition, reservation, or regret; even to you. All you have to do is take the gift and unwrap it to enjoy its contents. Each time you invite the Holy Spirit into your heart to have a conversation with God, either through His word or yours, He rejoices at the continued acceptance of His gift. God revels in this because He wants everyone to talk with Him and be with Him. But that begs a question. Just as we said in the opening of this chapter if God wants to do anything He can. So why doesn't everyone already love Him if that is what He wants?

Why Doesn't Everyone Love God if That's What He Wants?

Why go through the elaborate plan of salvation at all if you are God? Why not just create every man and woman to already love you and not need to sacrifice a Son to save them? God can do it if He wants to, certainly. He created such things as the vastness of space and all things in it, so why not just make us all love Him? Is it love if it is forced? Does it count as real adoration if we are all made to adore? Does the attention of an oppressed individual count for anything at all? The answer is no, it does not. It is not love if it is forced, nor does it count if someone is coerced into giving the desired response. God does not want robots worshiping because that is how they are programmed. God is interested in an honest response because the creation chooses to be near the Creator.

The Calvinists in the crowd are already warming up the predestined arguments, chosen and not chosen, and all the scripture they have that argue for a divine plan. I am a United Methodist, which means I follow Arminius who believed human beings are free to choose to accept God or turn our backs on Him. You can have hours and hours of Bible study fun if you look up "Free Will" and "TULIP" on the internet. These two search terms will reveal an entirely new theological controversy for you; however, that is not the goal of this writing. Suffice it to say, I mention it purely to establish where I stand, which is a proponent of free will. Do your own research on the topic and decide for yourself.

However, in the area of why God doesn't just make us all love Him, I believe it is because He is an honorable God. He created the rules the universe operates within, including free will; and He abides by His own rules. By the very nature of the Bible we have proof. God never once changed anyone's heart from what they were already inclined to do. Not one time did God alter a human choice that was made to suit His purposes. Yes, God hardened Pharaoh's heart but that was the inclination Pharaoh already had. God did not force Moses to go anywhere. God did not make Jesus sacrifice Himself and would have taken that burden away from Jesus had Christ asked it to be removed (which He actually did but then said, "...not my will but Thine be done.)

Scripture is full of men and women making choices. In each case they choose to follow the Lord's plan or step away from it whether they are aware of His plan or not. You have a choice now. You can choose to follow the Lord who desires nothing but good for you, or you can choose to follow your own desires. You have been well made. We have said that, so why not just follow your own desires, which are also for your own good, aren't they? The simple answer is that you have already been following your own desires to this point; and you have a longing for something more, something better than you have right now.

> [15] If it is disagreeable in your sight to serve the Lord, choose for yourselves today whom you will serve: whether the gods which your fathers served which were beyond the River, or the gods of the Amorites in whose land you are living; but as for me and my house, we will serve the Lord.
> **Joshua 24:15 (NASB)**

You can choose to continue to follow your own desires, and you will keep getting what you have been getting. But, if you want that something more that is nagging the back of your mind, you will have to choose a different path. If you want something greater than what you have right now, something more fantastic than you can possibly dream up on your own; then you must put yourself aside and take on His path (read Joshua 24:15).

This is Joshua speaking to the Israelites before they cross over the Jordan and take possession of the Promised Land. Today you have a similar "Promised Land" before you. You have chosen to deepen your relationship with God by talking with Him. His word intrigues you to the point you are at least considering reading the Bible if you are not already doing so. If you are not already studying and taking notes on what you read, you will someday soon because that is the pull you feel. If you want to get closer to that something greater you feel tugging at your heart, make your choice now just as Joshua instructs. Understand that this decision carries with it a burden. That burden is that when led to change your ways to His ways you agree to work to the best of your ability to make the changes, He identifies for you.

This is an honorable and worthy path you contemplate today. This is a life-long journey that goes to places of amazing things and astounding accomplishments. If this sounds like more than you are willing to bite off right now, that's okay. Just continue to talk with God as often as you feel led; but when you are ready, come back to this decision. How will you know when you are ready? The name Joshua, and the scripture from Joshua 24:15 will gnaw at you and worry you without letting go. You will find it comes to your mind unbidden setting your stomach to turning and make your heart uneasy. If these things happen, you will eventually make the decision, and once it is made things will begin to happen in your life.

Why does God want you on His team? Because not everyone is going to accept the free gift His Son extends to everyone through His sacrifice. For those who refuse the gift there is hope, if someone can connect with them whom they can identify with. You have lived a unique life lived in a unique way, and at the same time it is not so unique. There are thousands of people out there who have lived a very similar life as you with whom you can connect and identify. If you choose to follow the Lord this day, He can equip you with the tools to bring the message of the gospel to those with whom you can connect. If you can relate God's love to those other people just as you have discovered it yourself, they can be presented with the choice and guided into His arms just as you have been guided.

Accept the gift or not accept the gift. Make the choice or don't make the choice. Accept Jesus Christ as having sacrificed Himself to wash you clean or don't. But if you believe and accept Him into your life, you are in; and that is all you need to do to be saved. No complicated Bible study lessons, no intricate secret chants to learn, no meetings to go to, nothing else. Accept Jesus as your personal savior, and you are saved to go to heaven. Done.

More senior pastors, deacons, and bishops just got angry with me again. But it is true. If you make this one decision to follow the Lord God Almighty, maker of heaven and earth by accepting His Son Jesus Christ, you become saved at that very moment and are going to heaven with all those other Christians in the world. Yes, that one decision makes you a Christian, a follower of Christ.

God honors the system of rules He created. He allows us to make bad choices if we want just like He allowed Adam and Eve to disobey Him that first time in the Garden of Eden. The good news is that you are well-made by Him and He has a purpose for you to work on in His plan. If you are longing for that something larger to be closer to you and embrace you, then make the choice Joshua offers, this day. Just remember as you walk this road that the love of Christ is for everyone, not just you. That will be forgotten by some you encounter who may not agree with you. That's okay, because God wants to save everyone, and He has many workers He sends into the field to use many different tools to gather in His harvest. You are but one tool. There are others beyond you. If you make this choice with honor in your heart, you are ready for the milk of being a Christian, a follower of Jesus the Christ. If you do not make this choice today, ask yourself how many more days do you have between now and when you no longer can make this choice?

The Milk of Being a Christian

You are well-made. I know I've said that a lot, but it is true. God thinks you are worth dying for just as we've already said. You need to be reminded of this because it is a foundational principle of Christianity. All people are well-made and worthy of salvation, including you. The love of God is for all the world. On this one truth stands all the rest of Christianity that love is the foundation upon which all salvation is built.

The love of Jesus is the first concept to set in your heart. It is from this wellspring of love that all other actions must flow, or you should question your motives behind them. This is an important concept to internalize because the Bible outlines a large amount of behavior that God does not like. Just because you have made the choice to accept Jesus as your personal savior does not mean everything you now do is okay or approved of by God. You are still a fallen human being who has free will and can make bad choices just as easily as you made that good choice to follow the Lord. This revelation is not meant to steal hope, but to make sure you are grounded in realism not letting your guard down concerning bad behavior.

Those things God does not like are called sin. Sin is most often thought of as a theological term describing behavior holier-than-thou Christians don't like. The truth is the word sin comes from the archery world in ancient times, and it means "to miss the mark and so not share in the prize".

The English longbow was the most devastating weapon a man of war could carry around the time the King James Version of the Bible was being written. Made from the wood of a Yew tree and roughly just over six feet long the English Longbow devastated armies for centuries. The longbow was so important to the survival of England that every able-bodied citizen was encouraged to learn to shoot and archery contests were encouraged to be held at every festive gathering.

> [13] "The fear of the Lord is to hate evil; Pride and arrogance and the evil way
> And the perverted mouth, I hate.
> **Proverbs 8:13 (NASB)**

In an environment such as this the term sin came to be the predominant word used to explain how human beings fall short of the plan God has for us. Are there really behaviors God doesn't like? Yes, there are (read Proverbs 8:13).

Here is God telling us He hates a few things like being prideful, arrogant, or having an evil way about you. God hates these sinful acts, and there are other things God finds sinful as well detailed in the Old Testament of the Bible. We should avoid those things God doesn't like, but don't get discouraged as you begin studying the Old Testament for what God doesn't like. Remember that human beings are not perfect. We make mistakes and do things God doesn't like; we miss the mark of His idea for what is best for His creation. This is not the end of the world for you or me because Jesus' sacrifice to wash away our errors continues beyond the day He died and even past the day we accepted that He died for each of us. Jesus is our example of how to live according to what God likes. The Old Testament tells us what God likes, and the New Testament shows us how to live that way through the example of Jesus, the Christ.

If the sacrifice of Jesus paid for all the sins of the world before, during, and after His lifetime, why do we care about committing sin at all? Well, it is true that the sacrifice of Jesus paid for everything you ever did wrong, or ever will do wrong. That is an important foundational Christian concept to understand so let's stick with that for a minute.

The things we do wrong God calls sin. In a Christian setting when someone says a person is sinful it doesn't mean they are calling that person bad necessarily. What they are saying is that human beings have a tendency to offend God by doing what they want rather than what He wants. When we go against the wishes of God, we commit a sinful act. What Jesus did is to step before God and say to Him, "Here are all the things this person has done in their life, and here is the payment to set them right with you." Jesus bought our way into heaven on an individual basis with His own blood on the cross.

You've heard that statement before, but in light of the choice you've made, or are debating, it should have a new light. Why does sin, that which God doesn't like, matter? It matters because when we do things that God doesn't like; we are turning our back on His ways telling Him our ways are better. If we walk in our own ways declaring them better, God does not show favor to our plans, methods, or intentions. By our actions we separate ourselves from all that God has to offer us through working together in His plan.

God has a plan, the Big Picture if you will. His plan does not involve sin in the world. You can see the outcome of His plan if you read the Revelation to John (some call it the Book of "Revelations" but it is one revelation). This book of the Bible details how God's plan ends. If we wish to work to meet His goals and be more useful to achieve His aims, we must work to eliminate as much of those things He doesn't like, sin, from our lives. This is why it is important to identify and eliminate sin. We want to do a good job at whatever task God has for us to do, and we are held back from our best work by the things we do that He doesn't like.

So, you've made the choice or are leaning toward making the choice to serve the Lord. Why aren't things getting better? Perhaps they are and you just don't know how to recognize it yet.

Perhaps you are worried that given the troubles you seem to be under you're worried God doesn't find you approved to work in His plan? Remember you were well-made, we've already demonstrated that; but God loves you, too, even though things seem like He is punishing you right now. I can prove that one too (read Proverbs 3:11-12).

> [11] My son, do not reject the discipline of the Lord Or loathe His reproof,[12] For whom the Lord loves He reproves, Even as a father *corrects* the son in whom he delights.
> **Proverbs 3:11-12 (NASB)**

Once you have made the decision to follow the Lord things will most likely get a little harder or seem as though they do. Some of that is God pointing out the thing (or things) He would most like you to correct first. Other things of that may be spiritual warfare, which is real and which we will talk about a little later. For now, just know that God does love you. He wants to be in conversation with you, and He is willing to show you how to change so you can be more useful to His plans. Getting rid of the things He doesn't like in your life is one way to say thank you for the amazing gift that is Jesus paying the penalty for the bad choices you have made and will make in the future.

At the end of the last chapter we briefly discussed finding a church. If you have made the decision to follow the Lord, the task of finding a church will begin soon. I say it in the imperative because God does not intend for us to walk this path alone. In truth, we cannot walk this path alone and should not. You may not be ready for a church or feel you are not ready. That is fine. The media is rife with bad examples of organized religion, which I contend have been put out there intentionally to malign Christianity. However, for every bad church, bad church leader, or hypocritical Christian you hear about there are hundred-fold very excellent ones you do not hear about. Give those you don't hear about a chance to meet you.

The last scripture we read was Proverbs 3:11-12 pointing out God loves those whom He disciplines. The passage before that was from Proverbs 8:13 outlining how God hates pride. Perhaps there are those who need to learn a little humility out there concerning who is and is not in God's plan? If that is the case then perhaps their church is looking for someone to help them grow beyond the plans the human beings in it have?

[17] that the God of our Lord Jesus Christ, the Father of glory, may give to you a spirit of wisdom and of revelation in the knowledge of Him. [18] *I pray that* the eyes of your heart may be enlightened, so that you will know what is the hope of His calling, what are the riches of the glory of His inheritance in the saints, [19] and what is the surpassing greatness of His power toward us who believe. *These are* in accordance with the working of the strength of His might [20] which He brought about in Christ, when He raised Him from the dead and seated Him at His right hand in the heavenly *places*, [21] far above all rule and authority and power and dominion, and every name that is named, not only in this age but also in the one to come. [22] And He put all things in subjection under His feet, and gave Him as head over all things to the church, [23] which is His body, the fullness of Him who fills all in all.

Ephesians1:17-23 (NASB)

[13] For You formed my inward parts; You wove me in my mother's womb. [14] I will give thanks to You, for I am fearfully and wonderfully made; Wonderful are Your works, And my soul knows it very well.

Psalm 139:13-14

Perhaps that church needs to be turned back to God's plan? Or, perhaps that church is working diligently within God's plan and they need a laborer with your unique skills to help them move further down the path God already has them on?

Whatever the case, if you have decided to follow our Lord and Savior Jesus Christ, keep in mind He called twelve to serve Him, not just one. I know this is a longer quote but read Ephesians 1:17-23. This passage is pointing all of us who follow Jesus to organize ourselves under His leadership so we may better serve His purpose. Churches are supposed to place God's word first and follow His Son, Jesus the Christ, as their primary leader, hence the name 'Christian'. Those who gather in these churches are the saints referred to in verse 18. Jesus has been placed in authority over every earthly power. What this means is if you have made the decision to choose the Lord this day as Joshua says, then as long as you are true to what you carry in your heart a church should not be a scary place, but a place where you can grow.

But you may not be ready for a church, and that is fine. Just remember that when you have this gnawing hole in your walk with God, there is only one thing that will fill it. Keep in mind that God gave you power (read Psalms 139:13-14). You are wonderful and needed. Do not keep the treasures of your company and abilities to yourself much longer

36

for you have a purpose, and there is a need for you with your specific gifts out in the world. However, if you are not ready to begin the hunt for a church that fits you, God is big enough to continue to walk with you for now.

Chapter 4

Be Prepared to Change for God

A Decision looms, either freshly made or to be made, read Joshua 24:15 to remind yourself either of why you made the decision or what the decision is. By

> 15 If it is disagreeable in your sight to serve the Lord, choose for yourselves today whom you will serve: whether the gods which your fathers served which were beyond the River, or the gods of the Amorites in whose land you are living; but as for me and my house, we will serve the Lord.
> **Joshua 24:15**

the way, procrastination in this arena is not an option, because by definition not making a choice is a choice. If you are putting off actually saying to yourself (or out loud for that matter) which way you choose to go, and you think this is going to get you off the hook, God knows your heart. He knows who you are and why you do things. There is no use in trying to delay this task hoping that will "get you off the hook". You're not on a hook, you're living a life. Choose this day whom you will follow.

The good news is that while the church might be a place that doesn't feel right for you now, you do not have to go it alone as we've said. The conversation with God, Jesus, and the Holy Spirit can be had in the privacy of your own mind, for now. This doesn't have to change right away either but know that the church really is a safe place for someone who has a heart-centered on God whether those you are around have a heart-centered on God or not.

In reading scripture with a heart-centered on what God wants for your life, you are demonstrating a desire to change. Remember that while we are well-made and pronounced so by God (Genesis 1:31), we are also still in need of His guidance because we make mistakes (Romans 3:10). However, God knows we make mistakes, and He created a way for everyone to correct those mistakes through what His Son did for us all (John 3:16). The milk of the Christian life is based on saying thank you to God for the sacrifice He has made on our behalf to keep the conversation going. Some part or all of this may make you uncomfortable or you may disagree with it. That's fine, but you still feel that pull to something greater and you're willing to dig through things to find the truth. So long as you do so while talking with God, you will get there eventually, either to agreement with what I've said or something different. The good news here is that God doesn't do anything quickly, so take your time and do it right.

Do not take this statement about God doing things slowly to mean it is okay to procrastinate. God does not procrastinate; He takes His time to do things the right way. There is a big difference (read James 5:7-8).

We human beings tend to rush around. We are in a hurry to get things done, but sometimes when we rush, we get things wrong. This time, slow down. You can take your time, but you don't want to get this wrong. The difference between making a mistake and getting it wrong is defined by your willingness to make changes in your life based on what God reveals to you through your conversations with Him and through what is revealed to you by the Holy Spirit in your studies.

As the saying goes, some rubber is going to meet the road in this chapter. Some of this is going to be difficult to take in and agree with, but it is part of the foundation of a Christian life with a heart for God. Remember that God does not make mistakes. He does not do things wrong. His ways are what we strive for (read Isaiah 55:6-9).

> [7] Therefore be patient, brethren, until the coming of the Lord. The farmer waits for the precious produce of the soil, being patient about it, until it gets the early and late rains. [8] You too be patient; strengthen your hearts, for the coming of the Lord is near.
> **James 5:7-8**

> [6] Seek the Lord while He may be found; Call upon Him while He is near. [7] Let the wicked forsake his way And the unrighteous man his thoughts; And let him return to the Lord, And He will have compassion on him, And to our God, For He will abundantly pardon. [8] "For My thoughts are not your thoughts, Nor are your ways My ways," declares the Lord. [9] "For *as* the heavens are higher than the earth, So are My ways higher than your ways And My thoughts than your thoughts.
> **Isaiah 55:6-9 (NASB)**

Hard Decisions Lie Ahead

God does things differently from human beings. An example of how He does things is in the New Testament where we are told how Jesus lived the way God expects human beings to live. It is this example we are to strive to emulate in all things, and we can study that example by studying the Bible.

You live life a certain way, or you would not be reading this because you would be dead. The Bible is not a book to find justifications for how we are currently living. The Bible is a book to guide us in shaping how we live to more accurately do things the way God wants them done. As you study God's word you will find places where your life and how God says you should live will diverge. In those places you must focus your study time, because this is the leading of the Holy Spirit identifying something that must be adjusted.

Some people have the reaction that they are good people and don't need to change because they live a good life. They justify their continued living outside agreement with scripture in certain areas based on this idea. Keep in mind that once you have identified something you are doing that is not being done the way God wants it done, and you say, "I'm not going to change this thing" you are in effect saying your ways are better than God's ways. You cannot cherry-pick things out of the Bible and decide to agree with some and disagree with others and maintain integrity with honor. You can admit weakness in this area claiming an inability to change that aspect of your life, but this acknowledges the activity as not pleasing to God.

Acknowledging weakness in an area presents another problem though. By saying they are too weak to make the change, but they would if they could; they are setting themselves up to rely on God to make the change. Once you admit something in your life is not the way God would like to see it, you must change it, either by your own power or with the assistance of Jesus but change you must. How you change is another matter entirely.

Managing Change in Your Life

The first step in managing change in your life is being open to change in the first place. Having conversations with God in your head is a small thing so it is easy to do. Obtaining a Bible and reading it regularly is a little harder, but still easy to do on your own. Internalizing the words written in the Bible is simple too but acting on principles based on scripture is the sticking point for most people. Once you make the decision whom you will follow, you must conform to that leader or your decision had no honor or integrity in it, to begin with. There is no integrity or honor in a decision like this   because you are only paying that leader's ways lip service if you don't change your ways to match theirs. You can pay lip service to worldly people all day long and get away with it because people have no way to see into another person's heart for the truth of a matter. God doesn't have that restriction and knows exactly what your motivations are behind every action you take. Once you accept there is no hiding from God you can stop running because it's useless. Now the real work can begin.

First, not only are you made well because God made you that way, but you are worthy of the tasks He is going to assign you. This sounds simple; but, just like being well-made, being worthy is worth mentioning repeatedly. You have a unique set of skills God would like to take advantage of to further His purposes in the world. He doesn't need you. He *wants* you, and that is a big difference.

God wants you to be a part of His plans because He enjoys having you around for who you are, not for who you are trying to be. You change who you are to be more like Him because you think it is neat to be Him. This sort of change is difficult and takes time, but we said before God doesn't do anything fast, so the crockpot method of cooking is okay here. Living life is hard work, and it was meant to be that way, read Genesis 3:19. This is the verse where God punishes Adam to always have to work for his living and work hard. It is a truism about life in total that we must work at life if we are to honor the Creator so don't be discouraged when your changes don't go as fast or as simply as you think they will.

> [19] By the sweat of your face You will eat bread, Till you return to the ground, Because from it you were taken; For you are dust, And to dust you shall return."
> **Genesis 3:19 (NASB)**

The good news on these tough changes is that they can be done. Even those things you look at and say, "I just can't change that because I'm too weak", God has an answer for that too (read Philippians 4:13). Those people who are cherry-picking scripture to match what they already do so they don't have to change are doing so to avoid acknowledging this scripture. If they accepted all the things they needed to change and then admitted they can't change them because they are weak, they would have to rely on God to do it for them. This makes them dependent on something outside themselves, and that frightens them, offends them, doesn't ring true to them, or any combination of those statements. God is not leaving you to fend for yourself. He has said He will walk with you so long as you are true to His ways (read Proverbs 3:1-2).

> [13] I can do all things through Him who strengthens me.
> **Philippians 4:13 (NASB)**

> [1] My son, do not forget my teaching, But let your heart keep my commandments; [2] For length of days and years of life And peace they will add to you.
> **Proverbs 3:1-2 (NASB)**

> [13] No temptation has overtaken you but such as is common to man; and God is faithful, who will not allow you to be tempted beyond what you are able, but with the temptation will provide the way of escape also, so that you will be able to endure it.
> **1Corinthians 10:13 (NASB)**

We are weak creatures, and some of us know it. Knowing we cannot make the changes should not stop us from trying. We have a strong advocate with the Father in the Son. The Father has said in that Proverbs passage we can have good things if we listen to Him. We are told in another passage that we will not be tempted beyond our ability to resist without also being given a way out (read 1 Corinthians 10:13).

God wants us to improve. He wants us to be with Him. He wants us to have a better life, and He has given us a way to accomplish all that and more if we will just listen to Him. You are talking *to* God, but now is the time to start learning to listen as well while you make changes to your life. If you will listen to Him He will help you map out the changes that need to be made and walk with you through those changes.

The Path of Change

Your path of change is going to be different or have some different aspects to it. The things God shows you to change may be similar to someone else, but the way you do it will be decidedly personal. Make sure you are centered on the idea that what you have to address is not necessarily what someone else needs to address. The danger here is assuming everyone else has a problem with this issue too (read Romans 14:13).

This passage is good advice in all things where you find God leading you. For that matter, the things you decide the Bible is telling you may be for very personal change and not apply to anyone beyond yourself. Make sure the things you feel are from God do not become a stumbling

> [13] Therefore let us not judge one another anymore, but rather determine this— not to put an obstacle or a stumbling block in a brother's way.
> **Romans 14:13 (NASB)**

block for someone else who may not have trouble with the thing you are dealing with.

Another area of caution to be concerned about when you begin making changes directed by God is not to look too far ahead. Sometimes human beings want to lay out a long-range plan, map out all the steps from where we are to the finish line. This is prudent in many areas of life, but when walking on God's path deciding which stones to step on down the road is not always wise. Looking too far into the future and deciding where God wants me to go many times leads us down our path and not God's path. For the time being it is best to focus on the step directly in front of you and perhaps the next step but no further. Over time you will get better at seeing where God's path is leading, but for now stick closer to the immediate future.

As you make your decisions about where to step next, it is a really good idea to consult with wise counsel about your plans. I know church doesn't feel right at the moment, and it doesn't have to, for now. Wise counsel doesn't have to mean church. In fact, if you do not have a church right now, you don't know if the people in that building are wise or not. Wise counsel is merely someone who has had a good outcome in their life, walked a similar path as you, and has the wisdom born of experience to pass on. If you don't have this type of person in your life right now your first step in this path of change is to have a conversation with God about finding such a person.

If you do not currently have anyone in your life you consider to be 'wise counsel' then let me suggest you allow God to direct your path. Having this person in your life will be a very useful resource. If you trust God to guide you, then here is my suggestion on how to find that first wise counsel.

First, have a short conversation with God and ask Him to either direct you to this person or direct that person to you. After you ask Him for this, you must be vigilant and perceptive for the leadings of the Holy Spirit. Be patient though, because remember God doesn't do things quickly.

Second, I have tossed out the idea of finding a church several times. Each time I've mentioned it you have either begun listing reasons to avoid that building or thoughts of which church might fit the bill have entered your head. Let me suggest that if there is a church in your area that has given you no reason to dislike it, has perhaps come to mind once or twice, and you find you are constantly taking note of its presence; then perhaps you should stop in and talk with them? This is a scary prospect for some, but it shouldn't be. Let's talk a bit about how the introduction at a new church might work.

Churches have things going on all the time, not just on Sunday as many people think. However, a random day of the week is not usually the best time to just 'drop in'. The simplest approach is to read their sign for times when Sunday services are held or go on their website for the same information. Then, pick a Sunday (this coming Sunday would be good) and go to church.

I know going to church on Sunday sounds risky, but it really isn't and here's why. First, there are lots of other people going there too at this time because Sunday is the busiest time of the week for any church, and it is easy to get lost in the crowd on a Sunday. Second, the people you are most concerned about, the senior pastor and other ministers, are very busy at this time and while they will be friendly and welcoming, do not have much time for a long conversation. Lastly, they will not chase you down if you decide to leave because they have other duties on Sunday that require them to stay, though that is not to imply they would chase you down any other day either.

A good church will have many friendly congregants who will greet you and speak to you as you enter and sit in the service. Chances are they will recognize that you are new and mention it. There is no cause for alarm and dealing with this is simple. Just smile and say, "Yes, I'm just looking for a church home," or "I'm just visiting today." They may then begin to tell you about the wonderful Bible studies they have there, invite you to their Sunday school class (no, this is not just for the little children), or even a meal that afternoon. Some folks may just welcome you and leave you alone. The bottom line is that this gives you an opportunity to visit a church with little risk.

The advantages of visiting on Sunday are many. You get to see what the makeup of the congregation looks like. You get to meet as many of those people as you like. If you don't want to meet anyone short, polite responses usually get the message across. However, if they are persistent you can always leave with little or no consequence.

I would not suggest just leaving though. You worked up the courage to step inside the building, and it does take courage to do that for the first time, or the first time in a while. You will have a better feeling about the event as a whole if you stick it out to the end of the service. Plus, the person you really want to meet is whoever is presenting the message that day, and that person will be at the door shaking hands with everyone as you leave. While this is a poor time to choose for a long conversation with that person, a short sentence or two letting them know you are looking for a church home is not out of order. If you do say this, they will most likely ask you to stick around until everyone has left the service for a longer conversation. Feel free to decline this invitation if you are not ready for that discussion yet but know they will be looking for you next Sunday if they are the regular pastor of that church. Should you make that statement and they say nothing perhaps this is not the right place for you or perhaps a different person is the one to whom you should be talking?

Why am I suggesting this step if church is something you are opposed to? I suggest this step because, if you are going to mature as a Christian in a manner consistent with biblical teachings, you will eventually need a church home and have to find one. If you do not have someone in your life you consider 'wise counsel' then this is a good first step to finding one, but how do you know who to trust? You don't until you talk to them and try. That is why I am suggesting you visit a church on Sunday because the wisest people in the ways of God and the

Bible generally are found in churches. Keep in mind that churches are filled with human beings, too, so there are some (remember the 10% we talked about) who are not wise inside churches. Just decide not to associate with the ones who do not treat you well. If the whole church seems to not treat you well then find another and repeat the process. There is a church that is right for you out there, I promise.

To recap how to find wise counsel, have a conversation with God first. Be specific with God about what you are looking for in a church too, He will listen though He will not provide something that is against what He thinks is good. Next, study some in the Bible about what you are looking for in the people at this church so you can recognize it. Third, go to a Sunday service to see who is in this church and how they treat you. Finally, talk to these people to see what kind of folks attend this church because you don't know who they are by looking at them just as they don't know who you are by looking at you.

If you do these things you can find someone you can trust and rely on to give you wise counsel. You may not find that person right off, and you may even trust a few people who let you down. However, as long as you start by trusting God, He will walk with you through this protecting you as you go. If you're not sure what or how to ask God to help you in this effort, just remember the prayer Jesus taught His disciples in Matthew 6:7-13 and pray that way. God will listen.

Justifying Your Ways is Not What the Bible is For

Here is a hard truth of a Christian way of life. The Bible is not there to be used as a proof-text to tell you why what you are doing is right. While I have said many times, and will say many more times that you are well-made, not everything you do is considered good by God. There is a simple rule I use to determine when something I'm doing needs to be changed to God's ways. If I am searching the scriptures to find reasons, why my behavior is okay or trying to justify what I am doing is right, then I am usually avoiding the difficult notion that I need to change. But what is 'justifying'?

Justifying is the act of looking for support for current actions. Human beings tend to want to be right. You and I both want to be able to say, "I'm doing it right. Hurray for me!" So, we go to God's word looking for things that tell us what we are doing is okay with God. Sometimes we find scripture that says, "And God said action A is right and good in His sight." However, usually, we find scripture that appears ambiguous toward action A, so we begin a monologue in our head. As we carry on this running conversation with ourselves, we try to bend and twist the scriptures we've found relating to Action A to meet what we *hope* God thinks about it. This is justifying.

Justifying is not good for us because we are avoiding the hard truth that we need to change what we are doing. Justifying usually occurs because the change we know we should make is difficult, and we don't want to go to the effort. The truth is the Holy Spirit has made something plain to us through our reading of the Bible, and we are avoiding that understanding willfully because we don't want to change.

Once you have identified this situation some difficult internal discussions are ahead. First, you must stop the justifying. Justifying is destructive and not constructive. In the beginning it will be hard to stop the downward spiral of justification.

Next, have a conversation with God about the situation and ask Him to guide you. If you have identified someone whom you consider 'wise counsel' in your life perhaps a conversation about the potential change is needed to guide you as well.

Finally, open up to the change and identify a first step to making the change come about. You don't have to switch the behavior overnight, but if you have truly made the decision to follow the Lord, then this change is inevitable. By not taking that first step now you are only delaying moving further down God's path. Instead of fighting the change, embrace it so you can rush to the things God is preparing for you. You will not understand how wonderful those new things are until you experience them for the first time, but they are wonderful.

Grounding Change in the Word of God

There is a cautionary statement about these changes. The source of proposed change can come from many different sources. Regardless of where the idea for a change in your life comes from, make sure it is rooted firmly in God's word as contained in the Bible. Since I'm telling you to start there, I will start there as well. Read 2 Timothy 3:16-17.

The Bible is good to learn from. The Bible prepares you for *every* good work. However, be careful not to read scripture out of context or in a vacuum. How do you read scripture in context? There are a few points you have to make sure you check off as you study scripture to make sure you have the full meaning being imparted. Often a single scripture captures your attention as implying a meaning, and you look it up to see it for yourself. When this occurs make sure you know the following things about that scripture before you file it away as 'understood'.

> [16] All Scripture is inspired by God and profitable for teaching, for reproof, for correction, for training in righteousness; [17] so that the man of God may be adequate, equipped for every good work.
> **2 Timothy 3:16-17 (NASB)**

First, know who is speaking. Move both up and down from the passage until you can identify the person who is speaking, or for whom they are speaking. Second, make sure you have all the scripture that encompasses the entire idea of what is being presented such as cause and effect or the concept. Finally, read until you can identify to whom the speaker is addressing the comments, or for whom they are being said. Once you know who is speaking, to whom they are talking, and what they are talking about, you have ninety percent of the context about a scriptural passage. The other 10% comes from digging into things like biblical histories, commentaries, Greek interlinear translations, and other reference books.

Once you have the context of a passage you can spend some time thinking about its meaning. Make sure you take what you have read and see how it fits into the other scripture you already understand. For new truths you believe have been revealed make sure you consult other sources such as that 'Wise Counsel' we spoke of, as well as historical understandings like biblical commentaries. There have been more atrocities committed in the name of God, both intentional and unintentional because someone took a single scripture out of context or didn't ask questions about what they thought the Holy Spirit revealed to them.

Change can be difficult. The good news is it gets easier the more you do it. Change can also be frightening and scary, but it doesn't have to be that way. Remember you have the Creator of the universe, His Son, and their Best Friend walking along with you. If you keep your heart in God's word and His ways, you can rest assured He will look out for you along the way.

God reveals things to His children through the Holy Spirit as we diligently study His Word. Take advantage of the information He has given you. Do not resist the changes He proposes because they are to improve your life, not make it worse. Some of those changes may seem hard or make little sense initially but you have to trust God. He is patient, as we've said. He has a purpose for you, and He has a need for your input into life. Start down that road of change He has identified for you so you can get to the wonderful things He has waiting for you when you are ready.

People who have gone through these changes know it is difficult. The Twelve Step programs everywhere are designed around making change as easy as it can be. One of the truths those programs know and realize is that a good support group of like-minded people goes a long way to making the change manageable. The Christian support group has many names; Sunday School Class, Bible Study Group, Small Group, Fellowship, Accountability Group, Men's Club, Sewing Circle, and many more. All these groups are found in churches very easily and in large numbers.

You may be rolling your eyes at me because you feel I am pounding joining a church again. I am, but I'm also aware you may not feel you are ready for that level of change. Just keep talking with God, listening to His leadings, studying His word, and thinking about the meaning He is revealing to you. When He wants you to be involved with other Christians, you will be and not one moment sooner. Because He knows you and knows how much you can handle, He won't put more on you than you can deal with. Remember that passage from Philippians about how you can do anything because you walk with the one who can strengthen you to handle it? That is true here as well.

You may have already found a church, or you may have decided you are never going to set foot in a church as I did. I can assure you if you make the decision to follow the Lord, and honor it, you will go wherever He directs you, even to church, just as I did. Regardless of the mindset you find yourself in begin your studies of His word in earnest now.

Once you do, begin reading God's word with the heart to accept what He reveals there, the world shifts in amazing ways.

Keep in mind that biblical study has been around for over two thousand years. What you are reading has been read, thought about, debated, and ruminated over countless times before you even appeared on the earth. Others have written down their opinions on every aspect of the Bible and what it means. Some are good, and some are not so good, but take advantage of it all to expand what you know about what He says about life.

Do not accept contradictions in the scripture, or what appears as a contradiction to you. This is just something you haven't studied long enough to understand and fit into the whole of creation. Some of those things may never fit or be understood until you meet God and get to talk with Him about it. However, for those things that do appear contradictory, spend some time studying them so you can make an attempt to fit them into the whole of scriptural understanding.

Do accept controversy about what you believe is in the Bible. Many of the truths God has contained in His word are not things people want to hear. If God's call on you has revealed difficult things, be willing to step forward into that challenge. However, make sure you step forward with a heart of love from wise counsel and in full understanding of scripture as a whole. As long as opponents want to discuss their opposing views with you from a scriptural standing, and you have your basis in scripture, everything will be in His hands.

This is the final assurance. If you discuss scripture with other people from the standpoint of learning more rather than winning an argument, you cannot fail. If you have begun to accept change in your life trying diligently to shift into a more acceptable way of living that is approved of by God, you are on the right path. Read 2 Timothy 2:15. Ground everything you believe in scripture and you are building upon the solid rock of salvation and the foundation laid for you with the cornerstone that was rejected.

> [15] Be diligent to present yourself approved to God as a workman who does not need to be ashamed, accurately handling the word of truth.
> **2 Timothy 2:15 (NASB)**

Chapter 5

The Milk and the Meat: Maturing Your Christianity

That relentless tug to something greater is still there, I know. You still feel the pull to be more than you are but you're not sure how to get there. You sit alone reading, writing things down (or not), pondering; and all that comes out of it, for the most part, are more questions. The lack of answers is sometimes frustrating, yes. Perhaps you are coming up with answers, but they feel imperfect, incomplete, or not whole. I know this feeling well, and I can tell you how to soothe that feeling, but you will not like my answer.

> [13] For everyone who partakes *only* of milk is not accustomed to the word of righteousness, for he is an infant. [14] But solid food is for the mature, who because of practice have their senses trained to discern good and evil.
> **Hebrews 5:13-14 (NASB)**

Before I give you that answer, think on this passage: Hebrews 5:13-14. I hope that by now you are convinced you are a well-made person. Scripture is for you and does contain answers even though some seem to have failed you or feel incomplete to this point. The choice looms before you like that flimsy spider web filled with morning dew that bars your way down a forest trail. You know the web is no real obstacle to your path, but you stare at it rooted to the spot.

The choice, like that spider web has become a real obstacle to you progressing down the path to your destination, as real as any wall ever erected. You feel like you will have to give up all the things you enjoy and take on a bunch of rules that sap the joy out of life. Nothing I can say will remove that feeling, I know because I have felt that way, too.

The church has become, for you, an obstacle to getting to Jesus because of the flawed and fallen human beings you have encountered there before. Their lives have not presented a picture that matches the words they have spoken, and you do not want to be associated with that. Such hypocrisy jars you to your core, and the idea of being lumped in with it has moved you further away from it, but I am here to tell you now it isn't that way in all places.

Hypocrisy exists in the church just as it does in any place where humans congregate; but so, does Love, so does kindness, so does hope. Do not paint all Christians with the brush of the hypocritical few you have encountered to this point. There is a group of them out there just like you who know you, understand you, and can connect with you on a level you are looking for. Perhaps you are not looking for them yet, but you should. You will because you do not want to be alone.

You will look for these people because deep down in your heart, you long for others like you. You want to meet, talk, laugh, cry, and fellowship with souls who understand you just as you are. You want companions to journey down that path with you who have come from where you have come. The trick to accomplish this is two-fold.

First, wipe away the spider web of opposition to the choice of following the Lord (remember Joshua 24:15, reread it if you want) and choose for yourself this day who you will serve. We've already talked a great deal about that choice. Make it now. If you've already made that choice but still feel the lack of that understanding companionship you crave then the second part of this effort is for you. Second, decide to grow in your walk with God as much as you can.

This second part is not a call to giving up a bunch of things, but rather your growth with God will be guided by the Holy Spirit along His design for your life. This growth with God will only discard those things He does not want you to use for His purposes. Your unique life places you squarely in the path of a large group of people who will only connect with you. You are uniquely equipped to explain the love and life of Jesus Christ to that group of people. I cannot do it; they won't listen to me, but they will listen to you. I cannot reach that group of people because they see me as one of those hypocritical Christians who condemn them, don't understand them, and don't want them in my church. But they will stand shoulder to shoulder with you when they say this respecting you and your opinion. You can make a difference for them, not me.

This is a heavy burden but think back on the scripture in the opening of this chapter. Accepting Jesus Christ as your Lord, making the choice, is milk. If you do not feel that tug to something greater, a pull on your life by a power you cannot explain, perhaps all you are meant for is this milk of Christianity. Perhaps you are still waiting for that person who you can connect with to lead and guide you. If that is the case, stop waiting and look for that person actively, seek them as a thirsty person seeks cold water to drink on a sweltering summer day.

If the idea that you are immature or not ready for more offends or insults you, perhaps you are already growing in wisdom or at least ready to grow. You wonder what you must do to be ready for God to use you? Maybe you are not certain you are worthy of use, but I can assure you that yes, you are worthy. Change is something we've discussed already and growth in anything is change, learning is change. If you are ready to learn and grow in the word you must be prepared for the path beyond the spider web.

So, What's Next?

Yes, changes in your life are required to follow God, to be a disciple of Jesus Christ, because that is what it means to be a Christian. No one can be Jesus, but we can strive to be *like* Him. Our goal is to move our lives closer and closer to the excellent example He provided while with us on earth. What do you need to do to be ready for God to use you? You don't need to do anything.

The changes we've been speaking of to move your life closer to the example of Jesus are not in preparation to make you acceptable to God. Jesus' sacrifice has already washed away anything offensive setting you right with God, once you make the choice to believe and follow the Lord. If you are clean and not offensive to God, then what prevents you from being of use to God right now? Only you prevent you from being useful to God just as you are right this second.

The idea that the creator of heaven and earth cannot do something is absurd. Call to mind the single most amazing thing you have ever seen, most startling image of nature, or most awesome event you know. God made that, set it in motion, or directed it. The Grand Canyon was carved by God as an afterthought in creation. If He can etch that Grand Canyon in the face of the earth do you think He can use you as you are right now?

This state of use is also not dependent on anyone else. You do not have to wait for acceptance from anyone else. There is no one on the face of the earth from whom you must have approval before God can begin utilizing the gifts you have.

Right now, just as you are begin working for the Lord. He has a place for you at His table. He has things for you to accomplish. He has a cog in the machine of His design for the world you need to attend to, just as you are right this very second.

The changes we've spoken of extensively for which you are destined are not in preparation for receiving anything from God. The changes we've been talking about are to say thank you for the free gift of the salvation Jesus is holding out for you right now. This sentiment strikes some people the wrong way, I know.

Some people look at the totality of their lives and do not see anything to thank God for. They see hardship, burden, and work in their lives. I'm not saying you didn't, or they didn't have those difficulties. Human existence is difficult at times, yes. What I am saying is that making the decision to follow the Lord as Joshua did opens up the opportunity for God to shower blessings, good things, and joy in your life. Making the decision to follow the Lord is the narrow gateway to the Good Shepherd and all the wonderful things He has to offer.

The only examples I can give you on this are ones I have experienced or seen. As the car dealers say, "Your mileage may vary". If nothing else once you find a church you fit into, you are no longer walking alone because Christians surround other Christians in times of need with love, help, and kindness. When church congregations see people with a heart toward Jesus in need they reach out to help them. Sometimes that help takes the form of trying to correct bad behavior that is causing the troubles in life, such as teaching someone who can't manage their finances how to live on a budget. Another example would be the programs for substance abuse that are in churches to help people with that issue.

Clergy across the world are trained and taught how to be counselors in a wide range of subjects, and on those subjects, they cannot personally counsel you, they have a network of professionals to fall back on. Once you establish a heartfelt relationship with a church, they see you are walking with God, and you are hurting, they will reach out to help. Keep in mind though many churches are leery of those who are just trying to work another scam. As long as you have Jesus in your life, the conversation with God in your head, and the Holy Spirit with you in your heart the right church will embrace you in its protective arms if you will let them.

These things do not happen quickly. Doing things quickly is how human beings do things. God does things at a statelier pace. He knows the plans He has for you and they are for your good (read Jeremiah 29:11-14).

Trust in the Lord and He will take care of you. If your response to this is something like, "But what has He ever done to earn my trust?" then we may be at an impasse. God made the first move over two thousand years ago on a hill called Calvary. Later on, in your walk with God you may look back and see where He inserted His hand in a direct way into your life, but I can understand why you might feel abandoned right now. If you are having conversations with Him in your head right now though, then you have moved in the right direction, and He will begin to work with you for the better just as Jeremiah said He would. Just have patience for God to move in His time and not in human time.

So what's next? That is part of the amazing and wonderful discovery awaiting you. What is next depends on you and how you proceed. There is work for you to do in the fields God has sown for all of humankind. It doesn't matter if you are in the clergy or not, you have

> [11] For I know the plans that I have for you,' declares the Lord, 'plans for welfare and not for calamity to give you a future and a hope. [12] Then you will call upon Me and come and pray to Me, and I will listen to you. [13] You will seek Me and find *Me* when you search for Me with all your heart. [14] I will be found by you,' declares the Lord, 'and I will restore your fortunes and will gather you from all the nations and from all the places where I have driven you,' declares the Lord, 'and I will bring you back to the place from where I sent you into exile.'
> **Jeremiah 29:11-14 (NASB)**

> [22] Now flee from youthful lusts and pursue righteousness, faith, love *and* peace, with those who call on the Lord from a pure heart. [23] But refuse foolish and ignorant speculations, knowing that they produce quarrels.
> **2 Timothy 2:22-23 (NASB)**

work in those fields. You do not have to be called to be in, or already in, the clergy to have a harvest ahead of you (read 2 Timothy 2:22-23).

What's next? If you are not already in the clergy that passage presents simple, plainly spoken instructions for you to begin working on in your own life. This work is not to make you more acceptable to God. This is His suggestion about where to start in response to the desire you feel pulling you to something greater. If you want to fulfill that desire, see what that 'something greater' looks like, then begin here. For the clergy who might read this or those lay people who aspire to be clergy (read 1 Timothy 3:1-13).

This is a lengthy passage, but it is also aimed at a more mature Christian. This passage outlines the qualifications one should work toward improving if you wish to be in office in a church. If you have no aspiration for service in an office in a church this is merely a list of high qualities, you should look for in those who do want to serve in an office in the church. God set this bar, I did not, but it is there in plain-spoken words for all to see who wish to serve in that capacity.

[1] It is a trustworthy statement: if any man aspires to the office of overseer, it is a fine work he desires *to do*. [2] An overseer, then, must be above reproach, the husband of one wife, temperate, prudent, respectable, hospitable, able to teach, [3] not addicted to wine or pugnacious, but gentle, peaceable, free from the love of money. [4] *He must be* one who manages his own household well, keeping his children under control with all dignity [5] (but if a man does not know how to manage his own household, how will he take care of the church of God?), [6] *and* not a new convert, so that he will not become conceited and fall into the condemnation incurred by the devil. [7] And he must have a good reputation with those outside *the church,* so that he will not fall into reproach and the snare of the devil. [8] Deacons likewise *must be* men of dignity, not double-tongued, or addicted to much wine or fond of sordid gain, [9] *but* holding to the mystery of the faith with a clear conscience. [10] These men must also first be tested; then let them serve as deacons if they are beyond reproach. [11] Women *must* likewise *be* dignified, not malicious gossips, but temperate, faithful in all things. [12] Deacons must be husbands of *only* one wife, *and* good managers of *their* children and their own households. [13] For those who have served well as deacons obtain for themselves a high standing and great confidence in the faith that is in Christ Jesus.
1 Timothy 3:1-13 (NASB)

No Matter What is Next Remember These Things....

Never stop learning about God's word. I've said over and over you should get in a church. If you do not feel called to a church, don't go. However, don't stop talking to God. Don't stop reading His word. Don't stop learning from what you read. Don't stop improving your life based on what you learn.

Do keep talking with God. Do keep reading His word. Do keep seeking that 'wise counsel'. Do keep inviting His Holy Spirit into your heart to help interpret what you see, read, and learn.

> [5] Every word of God is tested; He is a shield to those who take refuge in Him. [6] Do not add to His words Or He will reprove you, and you will be proved a liar.
> **Proverbs 30:5-6 (NASB)**

Everyone you meet has something to teach you about the ways of God. No matter if they are Christians or not, they can teach you something new about God. Make sure you are open to what every single daily encounter offers you about the nature of God, Jesus Christ, and the Holy Spirit.

Understand also that while everyone can teach you something about God, not everyone wants to know what you have learned about God. In fact, some people are certain you have nothing to teach them because they know everything already. Be respectful of those people who are not interested in what you know. For now, the things God reveals to you may have to be kept to yourself. When He wants you to share what you know with others, He will make the opportunity plain.

When that opportunity does come to share, be ready. The best preparation is diligent study. Make sure you understand the material you study so you can discuss it thoroughly and accurately, read Proverbs 30:5-6. If you are not familiar with the material you may misquote or incorrectly represent it, and this is not a wise position to be in.

When the time comes be ready to share but don't do so from the position of trying to flaunt what you know or embarrass someone else by demonstrating what they do not know. Those who are interested in knowing what you know will ask you about it or draw out further information when you drop a simple comment into the conversation. It is at these times you may expand on what you know freely as long as you allow others to contribute to the conversation also. Don't turn a sharing opportunity into a monologue or no one will ultimately hear what you have to say.

Sharing what you know is important in the right context as long as you have the right heart to expand your understanding and wisdom. Do not share what you know to win arguments (read 2 Timothy 2:24-26). Arguing is not the right spirit because it is centered on building you up and not God by beating the other person in a war of words. If you think about some of those Christians who drove you away from God, many of them probably used God's word to beat on you about something they didn't like. This is not the purpose of learning what God has said.

> [24] The Lord's bond-servant must not be quarrelsome, but be kind to all, able to teach, patient when wronged, [25] with gentleness correcting those who are in opposition, if perhaps God may grant them repentance leading to the knowledge of the truth, [26] and they may come to their senses *and escape* from the snare of the devil, having been held captive by him to do his will.
> **2 Timothy 2:24-26 (NASB)**

We share what we know because we are interested in gaining wisdom, not winning arguments. If someone is misusing God's word share what you believe you understand from the position of expanding what you know. If they won't receive it then move on as God suggests (read Matthew 7:6).

> [6] Do not give what is holy to dogs, and do not throw your pearls before swine, or they will trample them under their feet, and turn and tear you to pieces.
> **Matthew 7:6 (NASB)**

Don't drop your pearls of wisdom before the swine of those who wish to argue with you. It is better to let God work on those people than argue with them.

You may not be ready for much more than accepting the conversation with God by yourself, in your head alone. If that is all you wish to have right now, then so be it. That is between you and God. Understand that just accepting the gift of salvation is the milk, the beginning of Christianity, not the end of it. If that is all you wish to do, you are shortchanging yourself of the grander blessings that spending a life walking with God can bestow upon a person.

However, if you hunger for something more, continue to move forward in what way you feel led. Keep your heart open to learn from everyone you encounter. Continue to ground your life in what you read in the Bible. Keep on changing to conform to what you learn so you grow in understanding and ability. Strive to meet the standard God has set for the laity and clergy in His word. If you do these things, a wider more amazing world awaits you beyond your very next step. Be willing to share what you have learned in the spirit it was given to you, and where not wanted happily moving on.

If you do these things with the Holy Spirit in your heart, Jesus by your side, and God leading you down the path, you cannot fail. Having made the choice to follow the Lord you have assurance from the creator of all things that His ways are good for you, if you will be mindful of them. He walks with you for evermore, and you never have to be alone again in any trial or tribulation.

Chapter 6

You Are Worthy

You are an amazing creation. We've been talking about how you are well-made; but you are not just that, you are amazing. Which makes more sense that you can breathe, walk, talk, and interact with millions of others like you, or you're just a product of random happenstance? You are not an afterthought or some random occurrence. You are not some errant pile of matter that happened to end up in the shape of you. God made you, He knows every part of you, and He has a reason for you to be (read Psalm 139:13-14).

This passage was written for you, but it was also written for every other person in all of creation before you, while you are here, and after you. God knows us all and has a use for us all if we choose to take up the challenge of that task. Everyone can enjoy the love and embrace of Jesus if they want. That is the message of the Gospel. No one is too lost to be saved, no one.

> [13] For You formed my inward parts; You wove me in my mother's womb.[14] I will give thanks to You, for I am fearfully and wonderfully made; Wonderful are Your works, And my soul knows it very well.
> **Psalm 139:13-14 (NASB)**

Someone in your past was presented or appeared as a self-styled 'Christian', and they did not represent Christ very well to you. This person picked up some attribute of yours they didn't like and tried to explain how it was offensive to God when what they meant was that it offended them. This person usurped the position of Jesus Christ on the judgment seat over your life when it was not in their authority to do so, and you ran from God because of it.

Now, even as then, you feel an inescapable pull toward something you cannot identify. In the past calling this thing that tugs at your heart 'God' or 'Jesus' repulsed you because you did not want to identify in any way with that person who so badly misjudged you before. So, Jesus was not an option, but you keep coming back to that as the only answer. Now, the prospect of being a Christian is something that you're toying with accepting, but the image of the person from long ago still haunts you. You still don't want to be that hypocrite, so don't become that person.

Become who God is leading you to be. Become someone so clothed in the love of Jesus Christ, so in tune with the acceptance, He extends to you just as you are, that you accept everyone you meet just as they are. Do not presume to move above your station and sit in the judgment seat of Jesus Christ as others before you have done. Move beyond those small minds to a greater understanding. Put down the glass of milk. Take up the fork and knife. Dig into the hearty meat of your Christianity and represent that meal well to those around you.

That tug that still pulls you toward something can be soothed. The longing in your heart for something more can be sated. Read the word of God in His Bible and discover the things He has written there for you. These words will fill an emptiness you may not know is in you until it is filled. Only the Word of God can take up that space in the void of your life, though you still may be running from that idea.

Run no more. Today, now, choose. Right now, make the choice or reaffirm the choice you've already made to follow the Lord this day. It is not something that is destined to happen, nor is it something inescapable. It is a gift that only requires you to accept and open it. Your motivations for doing so can be as pure as wanting to serve others from the holiest of positions or as base as just not wanting to take a chance on being wrong about eternity. Why you make the choice to follow Jesus Christ is irrelevant now. That you make that choice is what matters. The rest will come in time.

As time passes 'The Rest' will come, it has to; and you will want it to come. Your life will begin to change in subtle and not so subtle ways. You will change your life, or you won't. But change will be in your life whether you fight or accept it is up to you.

The easiest way to move forward with that change is to understand it. Learn about what is coming. Learn about everything around you. Learn, learn, learn. First learn what God says is good and bad, then learn what human beings say is good and bad. Then reconcile the two because they are rarely the same.

As you learn things will begin to appear before you as things you had not seen before. They were there before; you just didn't perceive them as you do now. The question is how you will react to them. Will you react well or badly to these new perceptions? We mentioned before that we are all, all of us well-made, just like you are also well-made. What you look for, you will find, so are you looking for strife and conflict or love and acceptance? If you look for good people, a good church, acceptance from those you encounter you will find it eventually. If you expect and seek intolerance, judgment, and condemnation from those around you, that is easy to come by anywhere. What have you been looking for in the past? What have you found to this point? What will you look for and expect to find in the future?

You have been granted a unique set of talents and gifts. They have been given to you to be used for a purpose. His purpose. You come from a unique background enabling you to combine those unique gifts and talents with that unique background to combine in a very singular way. There are people out there only you can reach who will listen to you because you are you. Others have been well-made in just this same fashion but with different talents, gifts, and backgrounds. Don't misjudge them or their usefulness to God any more than you want them to misjudge your usefulness. They have made mistakes as you have; they've just made different mistakes. Their mistakes are no better or worse than yours, and the reverse is true as well. God loves both of you and has a purpose for both of you. Don't just let that other person fulfill his or her purpose for God, *help them fulfill their purpose for God.*

> 7 " Do not judge so that you will not be judged. ² For in the way you judge, you will be judged; and by your standard of measure, it will be measured to you. ³ Why do you look at the speck that is in your brother's eye, but do not notice the log that is in your own eye? ⁴ Or how can you say to your brother, 'Let me take the speck out of your eye,' and behold, the log is in your own eye? ⁵ You hypocrite, first take the log out of your own eye, and then you will see clearly to take the speck out of your brother's eye.⁶ " Do not give what is holy to dogs, and do not throw your pearls before swine, or they will trample them under their feet, and turn and tear you to pieces.
> **Matthew 7:1-6 (NASB)**

I am guilty of sins you are not. You have done some things I have not done. I do not wish to receive a fair trial because in all honesty, if I get what I deserve from God for what I have done hope is already lost, because I have not been a nice person. I am not interested in receiving fairness when it comes time for my judgment. I want mercy, I need mercy, and Jesus assures me I will get mercy if I will give it (read Matthew 7:1-6).

The author of fairness assures me I will receive from Him just as I give others. That being the case, my fate is in my own hands. If I offer you the mercy I wish to receive, I shall have it. If I offer you condemnation, then that is what I shall have as well.

You are no different than I am. While what you have done through the course of your life is unique to you, the situation is the same. God made you well, but you have made some mistakes in your life for which you need mercy. Will you give others that same courtesy you are requesting from God? You control how you will be judged so make your decisions wisely. Do not ask for justice upon others unless you are ready to receive justice for everything you have done as well.

This is not a Universalist approach to salvation by any stretch. I believe the Bible is quite clear on this subject that Jesus Christ is the only way to enter into heaven. However, I am not the gatekeeper of heaven. I am but a fallen reader of the perfect word of God, which causes imperfect understanding many times. Fortunately for all of creation the gates of heaven are not mine to open and shut. That task rests with Jesus Christ who has a heart for the job. It is with Him that the job of judging the actions of all mankind rests, and that is a most comforting thought.

Our task, yours and mine, as imperfect readers of the word, is to affect the lives of as many people as we can in a positive way for God. We must help as many people as we can either start or continue their conversation with God. Every action we take should be oriented toward the goal of either introducing someone to that conversation or continuing that conversation toward its ultimate concluding embrace with God (read Matthew 9:37-38).

> 37 Then He said to His disciples, "The harvest is plentiful, but the workers are few. 38 Therefore beseech the Lord of the harvest to send out workers into His harvest."
> **Matthew :37-38 (NASB)**

Whether you sowed the seeds, weeded the fields, watered the plants, or swung the sickle we are all involved in the success of the crop. Hinder no one who is diligently working in the fields at whatever task they are filling. Find whatever way you can to get the conversation with God started anywhere you can. When you find someone already talking with God, figure out if you are supposed to join in, listen, or simply ignore that conversation. Never, be found putting a stop to a conversation or you will have to answer for it in the end.

We talked about salvation through what Jesus did in chapter 3. If you don't remember the scripture I'm referring to, it is John 3:16 (read it now). That is a hope-filled passage, but I wish people wouldn't stop reading with that one scripture. Now read John 3:17.

God did not appoint Jesus to condemn people for their actions. Jesus' task was to save all mankind through His sacrifice. He did that (read John 19:30).

The task of becoming the perfect sacrifice for all of us has been completed. Our task now is not to judge people but to pass on the good news that a gift is waiting for them. Our job is to spread what Jesus has done for the entire world

> [16] "For God so loved the world, that He gave His only begotten Son, that whoever believes in Him shall not perish, but have eternal life.
> **John 3:16 (NASB)**
>
> [17] For God did not send the Son into the world to judge the world, but that the world might be saved through Him.
> **John 3:17 (NASB)**
>
> [30] Therefore when Jesus had received the sour wine, He said, "It is finished!" And He bowed His head and gave up His spirit.
> **John 19:30 (NASB)**
>
> [15] And He said to them, "Go into all the world and preach the gospel to all creation.
> **Mark 16:15 (NASB)**

to as much of the world as we can reach through whatever means we have been gifted, read Mark 16:15.

You met, saw, or heard about a Christian once who did not represent Christ well. Do not be that Christian. Be the kind of Christian you wished you had met back then. Go be that kind of Christian to people you identify with and represent God, Jesus, and the Holy Spirit in a way you would have reacted well to back then. Some will listen. Many will not. You do not know if you are a sower, weeder, waterer, or harvester to the people you meet, so just be who you are with Jesus in your heart spreading the good news of what your conversation with God has done for you. When you are rejected or cast down upon remember one thing. You are fearfully and wonderfully made. God pronounced His creation good, and that means **You Are Worthy!**

You Are Worthy
Sunday School Lessons
Introduction

"Fortune favors the prepared mind."
Louis Pasteur

Grace and peace be with you in the name of our Lord and Savior Jesus Christ. Thank you for being interested enough in the book *You Are Worthy* to investigate the Sunday school lessons written to accompany the text. You honor me with your willingness to explore the material deeper.

We will explore the following sections in this introduction before getting into the individual lessons. As the class leader I urge you not to skip this introduction as it contains valuable material to make facilitating a class easier and more productive:

- Goals and Intent of the book and lessons
- Lesson plans, layout and sections, and how to use them
- The roll of the class leader

Goals and Intent of *You Are Worthy* and the Lessons

The book *You Are Worthy* is aimed at people who are seeking to fill a void in their life but either aren't sure what it is or feel a pull to God but are resisting due to a perceived image of Christians and or the Church. The secondary and tertiary audiences are Christians who feel they offer no value because of things in their past, and new Christians who are struggling with things in both their past and present. For established and more mature Christians firmly on their walk with God there is still value to be found. Self-evaluation and introspection for assessment of current state is something that should be done from time to time. Even if the exercise is nothing more than to confirm assumed condition and direction, it is still good to have that confirmation.

The goal of both these books is to help the reader accept their inherent value to God, God's path for the reader, and God's agreement that there is value in each person's life regardless of that person's past actions or present circumstances. The statement "God doesn't call the equipped, he equips the called" is not always accurate. God gave each person a unique set of gifts. Each person has been through a unique life, and at the same time has shared experiences others can connect with. It is those shared experiences that establish a connection through which the Holy Spirit can use each individual to draw others to Jesus. The ultimate goal of *You Are Worthy* is to set people on the path God has for them to help draw others to Jesus Christ.

While it is highly recommended that each class participant have and have read a copy of *You Are Worthy*, it is not necessary given the nature of God and the Holy Spirit. These lessons are self-contained remaining within themselves for the most part. Where they depart from these pages, other reference material has been included to ensure a complete experience. Granted, these lessons are based on the individual chapters of the same name from the book. This means a more complete experience will be had by students who have read the book. As the class leader reading the source material is the first step in preparation for leading a class, so possessing a copy and having read it are prerequisites for being prepared.

Lesson Plans, Layout and Sections, and How to Use Them

There are seven lesson plans in this book. Six of them are based on the chapters of the same name from the book *You Are Worthy*. Each lesson plan is designed to highlight and focus on the concept of the chapter for which that lesson is named. At times the scripture within the lesson departs from and becomes an addition to the scripture from the book. This is by design. Where necessary, additional scriptural reinforcement is added to back up the stated positions in the text. This becomes added value to the lesson plans when used in conjunction with students who have read the main book.

The layout of each lesson is fairly rote. At the top of each lesson's first page below the title is a quote that reinforces the main concept of the lesson. Some quotes are from secular figures and others are from well-known Christians. In all cases the quote

---

[20]So he got up and came to his father. But while he was still a long way off, his father saw him and felt compassion *for him*, and ran and embraced him and kissed him. **Luke 15:20 (NASB)**

is designed to bridge the gap between the secular and the theological making the discussion more comfortable for those not steeped in church dogma, ritual, and tradition. Also on the first page is the lesson's guiding scripture passage. The quote and the scripture passage work in tandem to blend into the concept of the lesson. The rest of the first page contains background on both the person who said the quote and the book of the Bible from which the passage was taken. These entries are included to allow for a richer class experience for anyone to whom either the quote or the scripture speaks to, drawing them to know more.

Following the quote, scripture, and background is the lesson proper. The lesson itself is broken into questions to **Ask**, the **Point**, that is being made, and **Readings**, labeled in the order they appear. Each reading has been inserted in a sidebar box text as close to the point in the lesson as it can be inserted. This makes it easier to reference without page-turning and flipping. In some cases, the passage is simply too long for a sidebar, so it has been inserted in-line with the main text.

The final section of the lesson is the **Closing Statement**. This section is designed to be a summation of everything in the lesson. It is read out loud by the class leader. This helps to drive home the point of the lesson in case anyone is still unclear as to the lesson intent.

Sometimes, there are appendices after the closing statement to include word definitions in English, Greek, and Hebrew. These definitions are drawn from authoritative sources and not the whims of the author. The appendices may also contain other bits of information that are germane to the lesson as well.

The Role of the Class Leader

You have either chosen to lead a class, are thinking about leading a class, or have been thrust into this role against your will. In any case, you have a right to know and understand the expectations these lessons place upon anyone who will be in front of a group of people to discuss what is contained herein.

Be Prepared for Class. As a leader, which you will be while you present this material, you are constantly outnumbered.

[20]So he got up and came to his father. But while he was still a long way off, his father saw him and felt compassion *for him*, and ran and embraced him and kissed him. **Luke 15:20 (NASB)**

You will have a diverse group of people before you representing a wide variety of life-experiences. Questions will come at you. In many cases you won't have the answers, and that's okay as long as you are willing to acknowledge openly you don't know but will find out…and then actually find out, bringing what you found back to class. However, being prepared helps field more questions, so read the material beforehand. Read the lesson, read the chapter in *You Are Worthy*, read the scripture quoted; and where you are drawn by the Holy Spirit, continue reading. The more you cover before class, the more prepared you will be in class, and as Louis Pasteur said, the more fortune will smile on you to have answers readily at hand.

How to Prepare? Preparing means reading first and foremost. As stated above, preparing also means following the guiding hand of the Holy Spirit who will lead you to information that will broaden your understanding. Knowing what is in the lesson before walking into class means knowing what portions of the lesson connect with your own experiences. It also means knowing what portion of the lesson connects with the lives of the students in the class. Adding personal touches from your own life helps flesh out a lesson and adds to the classroom experience. If nothing else, this gives you an area of the lesson you can speak to with authority that can give you a refuge to go to so you won't feel quite so awkward if this sort of leadership role is not familiar to you.

What is Expected of the Class Leader? Everyone will be looking at you to move things along and keep things orderly. That does not mean talking over people or shutting anyone down. What it does mean is that they expect you to know what you are talking about. Reading the lesson material, book it is drawn from, and background material accomplishes that. No one expects a leader to know everything, but they do expect him or her to be informed and prepared. You will also be expected to keep the trains running on time. That means making sure you move through each section of the class at a pace that keeps things within the time you are allowed to cover the material. Each lesson can be covered in a single hour-long Sunday school class. It is the class leader's job to make sure that happens and to know

---

[20]So he got up and came to his father. But while he was still a long way off, his father saw him and felt compassion *for him*, and ran and embraced him and kissed him. **Luke 15:20 (NASB)**

if you have any class members who need to leave early for duties such as choir, ushering, or other tasks assigned to them. Don't rush through things but make decisions informed by the facts of who is in your class. To that end, making sure discussions don't ramble or get too far off-topic is a key duty of the class leader.

What You Should Expect of Students? You should communicate your expectations upfront to the class if this is not something you regularly do, or the gathered people are not a regular class for you. It is helpful for the students to understand what the class as a whole is expected to do. To this end, all students should be willing to respectfully talk to and listen to their classmates. Conversation and discussion is the life's blood of learning. That will be repeated later. What that means is that students will need to stay on topic as much as possible, and not ramble with personal side stories. This is a *very* fine line for a class leader to walk. Given how important discussion is to the learning process, and how rich that process becomes as people interject their own experiences in class, this is vital to being successful leading any class…it is also where the greatest risk lies. Make sure you are judicious in where you let the discussions go and for how long, but never presume to know better than the Holy Spirit. If the Spirit is leading class in a direction, you will neither be able to stop it or alter that destination. You shouldn't try either. You will have to use discernment to know when and if you should bring the class back on topic.

What Not to Do. Do not be the only voice in the classroom. The easiest way to draw students into the conversation is to simply stop talking and remain silent…for as long as it takes. Once the students realize you asked a question and really aren't going to say anything until someone else answers your question, someone will.

Do not see the lesson plan as ironclad. These words are suggested, but the Holy Spirit is the guide. Follow where the Spirit leads. If that remains in the lesson, all the better.

Do not be the only voice in the room for an hour. Learning happens when people are engaged. Engagement happens when people believe what they have to say is valued. Do acknowledge the contributions of others.

---

[20]So he got up and came to his father. But while he was still a long way off, his father saw him and felt compassion *for him*, and ran and embraced him and kissed him. **Luke 15:20 (NASB)**

Do not let any one student dominate the conversation. This becomes a two-person conversation with an audience, not a learning environment. Solicit other contributions with questions like, "Do you all agree or disagree with that?" then look around the room. If someone makes eye contact with you, ask them point-blank, "what do you think?"

Do not turn the class into a debate. This is not the forum to debate doctrine, social justice, church policy, or the latest news story. The exception to this is two-fold; if the Spirit takes the class there, *and* it is on topic for the point at hand. Otherwise, debates become contentious and polarizing. The class splits into three factions of those for, those against, and those who either don't care or wish to continue on topic. In any case, debating in class is not where the material is designed to lead.

Do not beat people up with doctrine or personal views. This should seem obvious, but as the leader you hold the bully pulpit of being able to speak when you want because you are "The Leader". Given this power, within the confines of the class it should not be abused by forcing personal views of the material on others. Certainly, present your opinion, but put that opinion on equal level with those opinions of the other class members.

Do not denigrate anyone's contribution to the class. This is where your position as the class leader requires some self-control. As the leader your thoughts have additional weight in many cases. Don't toss that additional weight around especially when it is aimed at someone in the class who is participating. Remember, the goal is to have other voices in class. If you begin tearing down someone else's opinion, that voice will shut down...or grow louder and lead to debating, which has already been covered.

Finally, do not lead this class if you in good conscience fundamentally disagree with the material. If you wish to debate the author on his position on any topic you can easily do so by visiting his website, emailing him, or locating him on social media. Contact information is located in the front matter of the book. What was written herein was done so at the leadings of the Holy Spirit and with no other purpose than to be obedient to the call the author feels God has placed upon his life. If you disagree

---

[20]So he got up and came to his father. But while he was still a long way off, his father saw him and felt compassion *for him*, and ran and embraced him and kissed him. **Luke 15:20 (NASB)**

with the contents you will not be a good witness to those whom God intended to benefit from these words. Please do not be a stumbling block to your brothers and sisters in Christ.

Recommended Structure of the Class

These lessons are designed to be successfully covered in a one-hour Sunday school class setting. Some of them may seem short for that time slot and there are a number of ways to fill time if you feel there isn't enough material there. What follows is a ***recommended*** structure for leading these lessons and is the structure the author follows in his own Sunday school class once a week with this and other material.

5 min Gathering: Gathering and fellowship
10 min Joys and Concerns: Go around the room giving everyone a chance to express anything they want to receive prayer for or express thanks to God for. As the leader, unless you have a secretary in the class, take notes on all that is lifted up here so you can both pray for it and/or send out a comprehensive list to the class so others can pray as they are led.
5 min Opening Prayer, Lesson Scripture, and Quote: Open with prayer asking God to be in the conversation and hearts of all present. Be brief but set the tone for learning. Next, read first the lesson scripture then the quote. In your preparations highlight any aspects of either the background on the quote and/or scripture that strikes you as particularly germane to the lesson. Make note of these highlighted sections here.
30 min Main Lesson: Cover the main lesson questions, points, readings, and discussions here. To help ensure you are not the only voice in the classroom, for each reading ask the class for a volunteer to read each of the readings. Try to have many people read. Be patient with those reading as some do not read as well as others. Take only volunteers for this. If no one volunteers, then read the passage yourself. If you are short on time and need to get on to the next point, also read it yourself.
5 min Closing Statement: Read the closing statement. This marks the end of the formal lesson unless you have something the Holy Spirit has placed on your heart to add.

---

[20]So he got up and came to his father. But while he was still a long way off, his father saw him and felt compassion *for him*, and ran and embraced him and kissed him. **Luke 15:20 (NASB)**

A keen eye will notice the above only adds up to fifty-five minutes. That is by design. The class will almost certainly take longer in some aspect or other. This gives you a cushion to make up for those areas that run long. If everything goes spot on according to the timetable, then your class has five minutes to gather their things and get moving to whatever is next on their agenda for the day.

This structure is not how you *must* run a class. This structure is how the author runs his class, and how the material has been designed to be utilized. Feel free to make adjustments as needed to fit your own style of classroom experience, leadership style, and timetable.

---

[20]So he got up and came to his father. But while he was still a long way off, his father saw him and felt compassion *for him*, and ran and embraced him and kissed him. **Luke 15:20 (NASB)**

You Are Worthy
Sunday School Lessons
For the Leader

"Give whatever you are doing and whoever you are with the gift of your attention."

Jim Rohn

You have either volunteered to lead, been conscripted, or are considering the act. For that, I commend you and thank you. Leadership of a Sunday school class is the single most rewarding thing I have ever done to date. I cannot express to you the personal value with which I hold the honor and privilege it is to lead the class I do. Give it some time and you will see those benefits too…if you apply yourself to the task.

What does that mean to "apply yourself to the task?" Well, in this case it means to give it the attention and effort it deserves. The Introduction laid out preliminary ideas, steps, and things to do or avoid that will aid in being successful as a class leader. This section specifically is going to break down some key points, additional research topics, and potential additional reading for each lesson. It is designed to give the leader added depth on the topic as well as additional reading material for anyone in the class who would like to know more. It is suggested that you compile your own list of information you used, for which you are most familiar to hand out either from this material or your own research.

Is this additional work necessary? No, it isn't. However, any class leader who does the extra work will find benefit not just for themselves but for their class as well. No one but you and God will know if you didn't do the extra work, but they also won't know if you did it either. This is not for accolades but is a tool to aid those who feel they would like to know more so they can be as prepared as possible for the class to come.

---

[20]So he got up and came to his father. But while he was still a long way off, his father saw him and felt compassion *for him*, and ran and embraced him and kissed him. **Luke 15:20 (NASB)**

Lesson 1: You Are Well-Made
Key Points
This is not about Righteousness. This is about value. Everyone has value to God, or He would not have sacrificed His Son for the sins of all people. No one sacrifices their child for things that have no worth. Righteousness is about being correct and in line with God. No one is in line with God always, but that same person is still considered valuable or of worth to God.

Additional Research
Dig into the Greek definitions of Made, Good, Righteous, Son, and World. Read multiple scripture entries for all of them and dig into the additional meanings for those Greek words. Look up the definition of Prodigal.

Additional Reading
Read the entire scripture passage in Luke for the Prodigal Son. Read at least one commentary by anyone on the Prodigal Son.

Lesson 2: You Don't Need the Church to Read the Bible
Key Points
People do not read the Bible. They come to church to be *told* what the Bible says, but they do not read it for themselves. Come to church, yes, but reading the Bible on their own is just as important.

> **Passage**
> [12] So then, my beloved, just as you have always obeyed, not as in my presence only, but now much more in my absence, work out your salvation with fear and trembling;
> [13] for it is God who is at work in you, both to will and to work for *His* good pleasure.
> **Philippians 2:12-13 (NASB)**

Additional Research
Select one or more passages of scripture from lesson 2 and compare them in two or three different Bible translations. Take notes on the differences and contemplate how those differences impact the lesson you will present.

Additional Reading
Spurgeon on the Christian Life: Alive in Christ by Michael Reeves.

---

[20]So he got up and came to his father. But while he was still a long way off, his father saw him and felt compassion *for him*, and ran and embraced him and kissed him. **Luke 15:20 (NASB)**

Lesson 3: A Personal Commitment to God
Key Points
A commitment is something that once spoken cannot be taken back. A commitment made to God is of
Additional Research
Copy Joshua 24:15 onto a piece of paper and carry it in your pocket for the entire week leading up to class.
Additional Reading
Begin reading *The Noticer* by Andy Andrews.
Read Ephesians 1:17-23
Read Joshua 24:15 you wrote out at least once a day in the time leading up to class.

Lesson 4: Be Prepared to Change for God
Key Points
A maturing Christian walk is one that is constantly not just changing but *looking* for that change to move away from the things the World approves of and toward the things approved of by God.
Additional Research
Research the early life of Winston Churchill and discover who he was before he became the leader of the United Kingdom during World War II.
Additional Reading
None

Lesson 5: Maturing Your Christianity
Key Points
The change from lesson 4 *must* be change to God, which means following God's word, not Man's. Maturing Christians seek God's approval, not the approval of the people around them or the secular world in general.
Additional Research
The additional research for this lesson is introspective, is digging inside one's self. Prayerfully and thoughtfully contemplate the things you hold as beliefs or principles in your life. Write them down and then figure out what they are based on? Then, try to find scripture that relates to these principles. Be

---

[20]So he got up and came to his father. But while he was still a long way off, his father saw him and felt compassion *for him*, and ran and embraced him and kissed him. **Luke 15:20 (NASB)**

prepared to change for God where what you've written you believe is different from the scripture you find.

Look up the definition of justify.

Ensure as you research scripture for your principles you are doing so to find out what God thinks and not to prove that you are right.

Additional Reading

My Utmost for His Highest by Oswald Chambers

Lesson 6: You Are Worthy

Key Points

You have value to God. Not that you are righteous or "holier than thou" but that God wants you in His plans.

Additional Research

Watch Brené Brown's TED talk *The Power of Vulnerability*

Additional Reading

Brené Brown's book *The Gifts of Imperfection, Daring Greatly, Rising Strong, Braving the Wilderness*, and *Dare to Lead.*

Lesson 7: Now What?

Key Points

Go. The key point for the last lesson is to take what has been taught and *do* something with it. Get involved in the church. Get involved with other people's lives. Get involved with God. Go and follow His path for your life and touch other's lives so they can catch fire and affect still others. Go and do, action verbs.

Additional Research

Research the life of John Wesley specifically, the Alder's Gate Incident in which he "felt my heart strangely warmed."

Additional Reading

Read the entire chapter of Romans 8.

---

[20]So he got up and came to his father. But while he was still a long way off, his father saw him and felt compassion *for him*, and ran and embraced him and kissed him. **Luke 15:20 (NASB)**

You Are Worthy
Sunday School Lesson 1
You Are Well-Made

"The best things are never arrived at in haste. God is in no hurry; His plans are never rushed."
Michael Phillips

Quote: Michael Phillips is a movie and film critic for various print media. He has guest-hosted Turner Classic Movies, regularly appears on podcasts, and is involved in a radio program celebrating music in film called The Film Score.

> **Passage**
> [20]So he got up and came to his father. But while he was still a long way off, his father saw him and felt compassion *for him*, and ran and embraced him and kissed him.
> **Luke 15:20 (NASB)**

Passage: The book of Luke is a Gospel that contains Narrative History, Genealogy, Sermons, Parables, and some Prophetic Oracles. The emphasis of Luke is Parables and contains more of them than any other Gospel (19 total). It is the third of the synoptic gospels. Luke, a doctor and a Greek Christian wrote it circa 59-61 A.D. He accompanied Paul on mission journeys, as described in the book of Acts, which Luke also wrote. The keyword in Luke is "Son of Man" which is used 80 times.

The key personalities of the book include Jesus Christ, His parents Mary and Joseph, the Twelve Disciples, John the Baptist, Herod the Great, Jewish religious leaders, and Pilate.

This book was written to record an accurate account *"so that you may know the exact truth"* (1:4), of the life of Jesus Christ as the perfect Savior of the world. He wrote to the Greeks to present Jesus in His perfect manhood as the "Son of Man," the Savior of all men.

This passage is from the parable of the Prodigal Son and includes verses 11 to 32.

First Reading: Genesis 1:31

Ask: Do you think this statement made by God, that everything He had made was very good, includes you? Why or why not
Consider: The Hebrew word for **Made** from Genesis 1:31 and the Hebrew word for **Good** from the same passage in the **Definitions** section for this lesson.

> **First Reading**
> [20]So he got up and came to his father. But while he was still a long way off, his father saw him and felt compassion *for him*, and ran and embraced him and kissed him.
> **Luke 15:20 (NASB)**

Ask: How do these two words relate?
Point: This is a value statement, not about righteousness. You are well-made.

Second Reading: Revelation 1:8

State: God was there are the beginning and the end, at the start of all time and when the last second ticks off the clock.
Point: God has seen, will see, and does see all things including you.

> **Second Reading**
> [8]"I am the Alpha and the Omega," says the Lord God, "who is and who was and who is to come, the Almighty."
> **Revelation 1:8 (NASB)**

Third Reading: Psalms 139:13

Ask: You are well-made, not good as in righteous but what is **righteousness**?
Point: See the Greek Definition for Righteous

> **Third Reading**
> [13] For You formed my inward parts; You wove me in my mother's womb.
> **Psalm 139:13 (NASB)**

---

[20]So he got up and came to his father. But while he was still a long way off, his father saw him and felt compassion *for him*, and ran and embraced him and kissed him. **Luke 15:20 (NASB)**

Ask: Is this for everyone or just a select few?

Fourth Reading: John 3:16 (NASB)

Point: Jesus' sacrifice was for everyone, not just a select group.

State: The parable of the Prodigal Son is amazing on many levels not the least of which is how God relates to human beings but note the Father's response to events in verses 21-24

Fifth Reading: Luke 15:21-24 (NASB)

Point: This is the reaction God has each and every time one of the lost returns to Him. This is **_not_** the reaction for something with no value, that is worthless. This is the reaction one expects when something priceless is returned.

Ask: Does the use of "son" in the parable mean only men?

Definition: Greek word for Son, Huios

State: Because God finds value in us does not make us perfect. Note Paul himself stated he made mistakes, but he also gave us direction on how to rectify those mistakes

Sixth Reading: Romans 7:15-16

> **Fourth Reading**
> [16] For God so loved the world, that he gave his only begotten Son, that whosoever believeth in him should not perish, but have everlasting life.
> **John 3:16 (KJV)**

> **Fifth Reading**
> [21] And the son said unto him, Father, I have sinned against heaven, and in thy sight, and am no more worthy to be called thy son.
> [22] But the father said to his servants, Bring forth the best robe, and put it on him; and put a ring on his hand, and shoes on his feet:
> [23] And bring hither the fatted calf, and kill it; and let us eat, and be merry:
> [24] For this my son was dead, and is alive again; he was lost, and is found. And they began to be merry.
> **Luke 15:21-24 (KJV)**

> **Sixth Reading**
> [15] For what I am doing, I do not understand; for I am not practicing what I would like to do, but I am doing the very thing I hate.
> [16] But if I do the very thing I do not want to do, I agree with the Law, confessing that the Law is good.
> **Romans 7:15-16 (NASB)**

---

[20] So he got up and came to his father. But while he was still a long way off, his father saw him and felt compassion for him, and ran and embraced him and kissed him. **Luke 15:20 (NASB)**

Ask: Where does Paul point us to find answers and solutions to the
Point: "The Law" as stated by Paul indicates scripture. Paul was pointing us to the Old Testament, but the New Testament is just as valid given it is all about Jesus' life and how to live out the Old Testament way of living.

Ask: Is God trustworthy?
Point: If God isn't trustworthy, then He isn't God. Because He is trustworthy, read the seventh and eighth readings in quick succession to hear upon whom we can call in times of trouble and a promise about those calls.

> **Seventh Reading**
> [15] Call upon Me in the day of trouble; I shall rescue you, and you will honor Me."
> **Psalm 50:15 (NASB)**

Seventh Reading: Psalms 50:15 (NASB)

Eighth Reading: Deuteronomy 32:4 (NASB)

> **Eighth Reading**
> [4] "The Rock! His work is perfect, For all His ways are just; A God of faithfulness and without injustice, Righteous and upright is He.
> **Deuteronomy 32:4 (NASB)**

Closing Statement
You are well-made. You have value, not just to other people but to God. You are not trash. These statements are not meant as hyperbole but as truth from the God of truth. His ways are not Man's ways. His ways are good and righteous, not to be put aside but followed. He has created a system that when followed blesses people. God and Jesus as one and the same (John 1:1-5) can be trusted because they were there at the beginning and the end (Rev 1:8) and they made it all (Job 34:4-6). Put your trust in God and your faith in Jesus. Follow the leadings of the Holy Spirit, and you will walk the path God has for you. You can do all this because God pronounced you well-made from the beginning of time and He thinks You Are Worthy.

[20]So he got up and came to his father. But while he was still a long way off, his father saw him and felt compassion *for him*, and ran and embraced him and kissed him. **Luke 15:20 (NASB)**

Definitions

Made/Asa

Hebrew Strong's Number: 6213
Hebrew Word: עָשָׂה
Transliteration: ʿāśâ
Phonetic Pronunciation: aw-saw'
Root: a primitive root
Cross Reference: TWOT - 1708, 1709
Part of Speech: v
Vine's Words: Create (To), Work (To)

English Words used in KJV:
do 1333
make 653
wrought 52
deal 52
commit 49
offer 49
execute 48
keep 48
shew 43
prepare 37
work 29
do so 21
perform 18
get 14
dress 13
maker 13
maintain 7
miscellaneous translations 154
[Total Count: 2633]

A primitive root; to do or make, in the broadest sense and widest application (as follows) :- accomplish, advance, appoint, apt, be at, become, bear, bestow, bring forth, bruise, be busy, × certainly, have the charge of, commit, deal (with), deck, + displease, do, (ready) dress (-ed), (put in) execute (-ion),

---

[20]So he got up and came to his father. But while he was still a long way off, his father saw him and felt compassion *for him*, and ran and embraced him and kissed him. **Luke 15:20 (NASB)**

exercise, fashion, + feast, [fight-] ing man, + finish, fit, fly, follow, fulfil, furnish, gather, get, go about, govern, grant, great, + hinder, hold ([a feast]), × indeed, + be industrious, + journey, keep, labour, maintain, make, be meet, observe, be occupied, offer, + officer, pare, bring (come) to pass, perform, practise, prepare, procure, provide, put, requite, × sacrifice, serve, set, shew, × sin, spend, × surely, take, × throughly, trim, × very, + vex, be [warr-] ior, work (-man), yield, use.

---

[20]So he got up and came to his father. But while he was still a long way off, his father saw him and felt compassion *for him*, and ran and embraced him and kissed him. **Luke 15:20 (NASB)**

Good/Tob
Hebrew Strong's Number: 2896
Hebrew Word: טוֹב
Transliteration: ṭôb
Phonetic Pronunciation:tobe
Root: from <H2895>
Cross Reference: TWOT - 793a
Part of Speech:
Vine's Words: Do Good (To), Good

English Words used in KJV:
good 361
better 72
well 20
goodness 16
goodly 9
best 8
merry 7
fair 7
prosperity 6
precious 4
fine 3
wealth 3
beautiful 2
fairer 2
favour 2
glad 2
miscellaneous translations 35
[Total Count: 559]

From <H2895> (towb); good (as an adjective) in the widest sense; used likewise as a noun, both in the masculine and the feminine, the singular and the plural (good, a good or good thing, a good man or woman; the good, goods or good things, good men or women), also as an adverb (well) :- beautiful, best, better, bountiful, cheerful, at ease, × fair (word), (be in) favour, fine, glad, good (deed, -lier, -liest, -ly, -ness, -s), graciously, joyful, kindly, kindness, liketh (best), loving, merry, × most, pleasant, + pleaseth, pleasure, precious, prosperity, ready, sweet, wealth, welfare, (be) well ([-favoured]).

---

[20]So he got up and came to his father. But while he was still a long way off, his father saw him and felt compassion *for him*, and ran and embraced him and kissed him. **Luke 15:20 (NASB)**

Righteous/Dikaios

Greek Strong's Number: 1342
Greek Word: δίκαιος
Transliteration: dikaios
Phonetic Pronunciation:dik'-ah-yos
Root: from <G1349>
Cross Reference: TDNT - 2:182,168
Part of Speech: adj
Vine's Words: Just, Justly, Right, Rightly, Righteous, Righteously
Usage Notes:
English Words used in KJV:
righteous 41
just 33
right 5
meet 2
[Total Count: 81]

from <G1349> (dike); equitable (in character or act); by implication innocent, holy (absolute or relative) :- just, meet, right (-eous).

---

[20]So he got up and came to his father. But while he was still a long way off, his father saw him and felt compassion *for him*, and ran and embraced him and kissed him. **Luke 15:20 (NASB)**

World/Kosmos

Greek Strong's Number: 2889
Greek Word: κόσμος
Transliteration: kosmos
Phonetic Pronunciation:kos'-mos
Root: probably from the base of <G2865>
Cross Reference: TDNT - 3:868,459
Part of Speech: n m
Vine's Words: Adorn, Adorning, World

English Words used in KJV:
world 186
adorning 1
[Total Count: 187]
probably from the base of <G2865> (komizo); orderly arrangement,
i.e. decoration; by implication the world (in a wide or narrow sense,
including its inhabitant, literal or figurative [moral]) :- adorning, world.

---

[20]So he got up and came to his father. But while he was still a long way off, his father saw him and felt compassion *for him*, and ran and embraced him and kissed him. **Luke 15:20 (NASB)**

Son/Huios

Greek Strong's Number: 5207
Greek Word: υἱός
Transliteration: huios
Phonetic Pronunciation:hwee-os'
Root: apparently a primary word
Cross Reference: TDNT - 8:334,1206
Part of Speech: n m
Vine's Words: Child, Children, Childbearing, Childish, Childless, Foal, Son

English Words used in KJV:
son(s) 85
Son of Man + <G444> (TDNT - 8:400. 1210) 87
Son of God + <G2316> 49
child(ren) 49
Son 42
his Son + <G848> 21
Son of David + <G1138> (TDNT - 8:478. 1210) 15
my beloved Son + <G27> + <G3350> 7
thy Son + <G4575> 5
only begotten Son + <G3339> 3
his (David's) son + <G846> 3
firstborn son + <G4316> 2
miscellaneous translations 14
[Total Count: 382]

apparently a primary word; a "son" (sometimes of animals), used very widely of immediate, remote or figurative kinship :- child, foal, son.

James Strong, Strong's Talking Greek & Hebrew Dictionary, (Austin, TX: WORDsearch Corp., 2007), WORDsearch CROSS e-book.

---

[20]So he got up and came to his father. But while he was still a long way off, his father saw him and felt compassion *for him*, and ran and embraced him and kissed him. **Luke 15:20 (NASB)**

You Are Worthy
Sunday School Lesson 2
You Don't Need the Church to Read the Bible

"A Bible that's falling apart usually belongs to someone who isn't."

Charles Spurgeon

Quote-In his book about Charles Spurgeon and reading the Bible *Spurgeon on the Christian Life: Alive in Christ* Michael Reeves writes,

> **Passage**
> [16] All Scripture is inspired by God and profitable for teaching, for reproof, for correction, for training in righteousness;
> **2 Timothy 3:16 (NASB)**

"...Reading a passage filled with explicit doctrine, we seek not simply to comprehend it but to be affected and altered by it. More than understanding, such reading involves transformation...

At its root, the transformation Spurgeon desired for readers of the Bible was a turning away from the sin that deadens and to the Christ who makes alive."

Passage-The book of 2nd Timothy is a Pastoral Epistle (letter from Paul to a church leader). The author is the Apostle Paul who wrote it approximately 67 A.D. and is probably his last letter. After Paul's release from his first imprisonment in Rome in AD 61 or 62, and after his final missionary journey (probably into Spain), he was again imprisoned under Emperor Nero c. 66-67. The key personalities are Paul, Timothy, Luke, Mark, and many others.

Its purpose was to give direction to Timothy and urge him to visit one final time. From the somber nature of this letter, it is apparent that Paul knew that his work was done and that his life was nearly at an end (4:6-8).

---

[20]So he got up and came to his father. But while he was still a long way off, his father saw him and felt compassion *for him*, and ran and embraced him and kissed him. **Luke 15:20 (NASB)**

Ask: Why should we read the Bible?

Point: This is not just another book to be read for a story or to say that you have completed the chapter, story, or book. This is an instruction manual from God that allows us to not just know what the Creator of all that is thinks but to walk with His Son through our own lives as well.

First Reading: John 1:1

Ask: Is Jesus in this verse and if so, where? If not, why not?

Point: The "word" or ho logos in Greek is Jesus.

> **First Reading**
> [1] In the beginning was the Word, and the Word was with God, and the Word was God.
> **John 1:1 (NASB)**

Second Reading: John 1:14

Ask: What implications does it have for all of scripture and life if Jesus and the word of God are one and the same?

Point: It means that Jesus wasn't just showing us how to live the way God likes, He WAS a life of perfection according to how God wants people to live.

> **Second Reading**
> [14] And the Word became flesh, and dwelt among us, and we saw His glory, glory as of the only begotten from the Father, full of grace and truth.
> **John 1:14 (NASB)**

Third Reading: Romans 3:10

Ask: If, as Paul says no one does good, how can anyone be worthy?

Point: Paul didn't make a statement of worth. Paul used the word "righteous" which is about moral decisions and actions and is not a value statement.

> **Third Reading**
> [10] as it is written, "THERE IS NONE RIGHTEOUS, NOT EVEN ONE;
> **Romans 3:10 (NASB)**
> Psalm 14:1-3
> Psalm 53:1-3

---

[20]So he got up and came to his father. But while he was still a long way off, his father saw him and felt compassion *for him*, and ran and embraced him and kissed him. **Luke 15:20 (NASB)**

State: It is not in the nature of human beings to make good decisions according to what God thinks are good decisions.
Point: Fourth Reading: Romans 7:15-16

State: Because Jesus is the Word of God Jesus showed us how to live righteously
Point: Fifth Reading: Matthew 5:17

Ask: If Jesus is the embodiment of the Word of God and lived a perfect life, and is the embodiment of righteousness what does that mean for us as fallible humans?
Point: All of scripture, the Old and the New Testaments are there to teach us how to be more righteous in our daily lives.

Re-read today's passage

Ask: What are the next steps for the Christian who wants to become a better person and is reading the Bible?
Point: Find tools, compare translations, and avoid troubles but first, pray without fear.

Sixth Reading: Psalm 23

Fourth Reading
[15] For what I am doing, I do not understand; for I am not practicing what I *would* like to *do,* but I am doing the very thing I hate.
[16] But if I do the very thing I do not want *to do,* I agree with the Law, *confessing* that the Law is good.
Romans 7:15-16 (NASB)

Fifth Reading
[17] "Do not think that I came to abolish the Law or the Prophets; I did not come to abolish but to fulfill.
Matthew 5:17 (NASB)

Sixth Reading
[1] The LORD is my shepherd, I shall not want.
[2] He makes me lie down in green pastures; He leads me beside quiet waters.
[3] He restores my soul; He guides me in the paths of righteousness For His name's sake.
[4] Even though I walk through the valley of the shadow of death, I fear no evil, for You are with me; Your rod and Your staff, they comfort me.
[5] You prepare a table before me in the presence of my enemies; You have anointed my head with oil; My cup overflows.
[6] Surely goodness and lovingkindness will follow me all the days of my life, And I will dwell in the house of the LORD forever.
Psalm 23:1-6 (NASB)

---

[20]So he got up and came to his father. But while he was still a long way off, his father saw him and felt compassion *for him*, and ran and embraced him and kissed him. **Luke 15:20 (NASB)**

Seventh Reading: Matthew 6:7-13

Closing Statement

The Bible is where God is, not in a human, a building, or someone else's interpretation of it in their book, but in your understanding of it. Read it and base EVERYTHING off scripture, not the word of Man. Reading His word is what guides us on His path for our lives. However, we cannot move down this path for long by ourselves. Eventually, other people will be needed to mature and advance our Christian walk. Why is this? Once again, scripture has the answer:

> [20] For where two or three are gathered together in my name, there am I in the midst of them.
> **Matthew 18:20 (KJV)**

<u>Seventh Reading</u>
[7] But when ye pray, use not vain repetitions, as the heathen *do*: for they think that they shall be heard for their much speaking. [8] Be not ye therefore like unto them: for your Father knoweth what things ye have need of, before ye ask him. [9] After this manner therefore pray ye: Our Father which art in heaven, Hallowed be thy name. [10] Thy kingdom come. Thy will be done in earth, as *it is* in heaven. [11] Give us this day our daily bread. [12] And forgive us our debts, as we forgive our debtors. [13] And lead us not into temptation, but deliver us from evil: For thine is the kingdom, and the power, and the glory, for ever. Amen.
Matthew 6:7-13 (KJV)

You cannot mature, seek wise counsel, or find Christ without other people. God comes first, and He can be found in the Bible, but to truly find Christ, live a Christ-like life, we need relationships with other people. This affords us the opportunity to serve others but to be served as well. Both serving and being served lead us to live as Christ lived. But once again, it all starts with God, and He can be found in the pages of His book, containing His Word, the Bible.

---

[20]So he got up and came to his father. But while he was still a long way off, his father saw him and felt compassion *for him*, and ran and embraced him and kissed him. **Luke 15:20 (NASB)**

You Are Worthy
Sunday School Lesson 3
A Personal Commitment to God

"When confronted with a challenge, the committed heart will search for a solution. The undecided heart searches for an escape."

Andy Andrews

Quote-Andy Andrews is a speaker and *New York Times* best-selling author of the novels *The Traveler's Gift* and *The Noticer*. The *New York Times* has called him, "someone who has quietly become one of the most influential people in America."

> **Passage**
> [15] If it is disagreeable in your sight to serve the Lord, choose for yourselves today whom you will serve: whether the gods which your fathers served which were beyond the River, or the gods of the Amorites in whose land you are living; but as for me and my house, we will serve the Lord.
> **Joshua 24:15 (NASB)**

Passage- The genre of the book of Joshua is Narrative History. It was authored by Joshua the leader of the Israelites circa 1405-1383 B.C. The key personalities are Joshua, Rahab, Achan, Phinehas, and Eleazar. It was written to assure the Israelites the Living God will reward obedience, and also record the entrance and conquest of the promised land.

Joshua demonstrates his faith in God as He follows the orders given to Him and takes leadership of the nation. Joshua truly was *"strong and courageous"* (1:7).

---

[20]So he got up and came to his father. But while he was still a long way off, his father saw him and felt compassion *for him*, and ran and embraced him and kissed him. **Luke 15:20 (NASB)**

Definition of Commitment

Ask: Why did God send His Son into the world as stated in John 3:16?
Point: Because He loved all of us enough to create a way to bring us all back into relationship with Him, both the gentile and the Jew. (For more on this read all of Ephesians 2.)

> **Commitment** noun
> com·mit·ment\\kə-'mit-mənt\
> **1a:**an agreement or pledge to do something in the future
> **b:**something pledged
> **c:**the state or an instance of being obligated or emotionally impelled.

First Reading: John 3:17 (NASB)

Ask: Does God *need* me, or anyone else, to accomplish His goals and desires?
Point: No. God is God and capable of accomplishing anything all by himself. Do you agree or disagree with this and why?

> **First Reading**
> [17] For God sent not his Son into the world to condemn the world; but that the world through him might be saved.
> **John 3:17 (KJV)**

Ask: If God doesn't *need* us, then why does He *want* us to be in relationship with Him?
Point: Love. **Re-read John 3:16 with emphasis on the word loved.**

> [16] "For God so loved the world, that He gave His only begotten Son, that whoever believes in Him shall not perish, but have eternal life.
> **John 3:16 (NASB)**

Ask: If God wants all of us to be with Him and love Him, then why doesn't God get what God wants?
Point: God is an honorable god abiding by His own rules. He gave us a choice and He allows us to make it just like He allowed Adam and Eve to make a bad decision in the garden.

Re-read today's passage from Joshua, but not as a passage of scripture, as an imperative choice for us today.

Ask: Do you think God is making a good decision when He seeks to embrace you in His plans?

[20]So he got up and came to his father. But while he was still a long way off, his father saw him and felt compassion *for him*, and ran and embraced him and kissed him. **Luke 15:20 (NASB)**

Point: Second Reading: Jeremiah 19:11 God knows what He thinks about you and it is meant to bring you good things.

Ask: How can God know that we will be good for His plans?
Point: Third Reading: Revelation 1:7-8. God is outside time and sees it all, the Alpha and the Omega, there at the beginning and the end.

Ask: How can God know us so well?
Point: Fourth Reading: Psalm 139:13-14. Because He sees and knows it all, He already knows you, who you are, and what you've gone through (and will go through) because He was there when you were made. He made you.

Ask: How can we be sure our participation in His plans is going to be worthwhile?
Point: Fifth Reading: Genesis 1:31. He made it all, from beginning to end inclusive of us all. Because He sees and knows each of us, He pronounced each of His creations as having value in His plans from the beginning and confirmed it when He sent His son to die for each one of us…because He loves all of us (**John 3:16**).

Ask: If we are committed to God and His plan for not just our own

Second Reading
[11] For I know the thoughts that I think toward you, saith the LORD, thoughts of peace, and not of evil, to give you an expected end.
Jeremiah 29:11 (KJV)

Third Reading
[7] Behold, he cometh with clouds; and every eye shall see him, and they *also* which pierced him: and all kindreds of the earth shall wail because of him. Even so, Amen.
[8] I am Alpha and Omega, the beginning and the ending, saith the Lord, which is, and which was, and which is to come, the Almighty.
Revelation 1:7-8 (KJV)

Fourth Reading
[13] For You formed my inward parts; You wove me in my mother's womb.
[14] I will give thanks to You, for I am fearfully and wonderfully made; Wonderful are Your works, And my soul knows it very well.
Psalm 139:13-14 (NASB)

Fifth Reading
[31] God saw all that He had made, and behold, it was very good. And there was evening and there was morning, the sixth day.
Genesis 1:31 (NASB)

[20]So he got up and came to his father. But while he was still a long way off, his father saw him and felt compassion *for him*, and ran and embraced him and kissed him. **Luke 15:20 (NASB)**

lives but the lives of all His other creations as well, what is the solution? What are we to do going forward?

Point: The "solution" is to choose God's ways over Man's ways, to commit to changing our lives to more conform like Jesus' life, to make the choice Joshua offered us in today's passage.

Re-read today's passage

Ask: If we are good people why do we have to change? Why can't we just keep going as we are?

Point: Sixth Reading: Isaiah 55:6-9 (NASB) God and Jesus are perfect examples of how to do it right. Their ways are the right ways every time were as human beings tend to make mistakes accidentally, make bad choices, or in some cases are just plain evil. God's ways are never wrong, bad, or evil. Ever.

Closing Statement

My hope for you today is the same as it was for Paul just 30 years after the passing of Christ (AD60) as summed up in a portion of his letter to the Ephesians. I can say it no better than this…

> **Sixth Reading**
> [6] Seek the LORD while He may be found; Call upon Him while He is near. [7] Let the wicked forsake his way And the unrighteous man his thoughts; And let him return to the LORD, And He will have compassion on him, And to our God, For He will abundantly pardon. [8] "For My thoughts are not your thoughts, Nor are your ways My ways," declares the LORD. [9] "For *as* the heavens are higher than the earth, So are My ways higher than your ways And My thoughts than your thoughts.
> **Isaiah 55:6-9 (NASB)**

[17]that the God of our Lord Jesus Christ, the Father of glory, may give to you a spirit of wisdom and of revelation in the knowledge of Him. [18]*I pray that* the eyes of your heart may be enlightened, so that you will know what is the hope of His calling, what are the riches of the glory of His inheritance in the saints, [19]and what is the surpassing greatness of His power toward us who believe. *These are* in accordance with the working of the strength of His might [20]which He brought about in Christ, when He raised Him from the dead and seated Him at His right hand in the heavenly *places*, [21]far above all rule and authority and power and dominion, and every name that is

---

[20]So he got up and came to his father. But while he was still a long way off, his father saw him and felt compassion *for him*, and ran and embraced him and kissed him. **Luke 15:20 (NASB)**

named, not only in this age but also in the one to come. [22]And He put all things in subjection under His feet, and gave Him as head over all things to the church, [23]which is His body, the fullness of Him who fills all in all.
Ephesians1:17-23 (NASB)

---

[20]So he got up and came to his father. But while he was still a long way off, his father saw him and felt compassion *for him*, and ran and embraced him and kissed him. **Luke 15:20 (NASB)**

You Are Worthy
Sunday School Lesson 4
Be Prepared to Change for God

"To improve is to change; to be perfect is to change often."
Winston Churchill

Quote-Sir Winston Leonard Spencer Churchill, 11/30/1874 to 1/24/1965, was by all accounts a mediocre politician at best before his rise to prominence during WWII. During the war he was instrumental in allied tactics, strategy, and mapping the road to victory. After the war Churchill was also one of the main voices alerting the world to the dangers of communism.

Passage-The book of Isaiah is Narrative History, Prophetic Oracle, and even a Parable (chapter 5). The prophet Isaiah wrote it at approximately 700 B.C. (Chapters 40-66, written later in his life approx. 681 B.C.). Isaiah is the first book in the section called Major Prophets.

> **Passage**
> [6] Seek the LORD while He may be found; Call upon Him while He is near. [7] Let the wicked forsake his way And the unrighteous man his thoughts; And let him return to the LORD, And He will have compassion on him, And to our God, For He will abundantly pardon. [8] "For My thoughts are not your thoughts, Nor are your ways My ways," declares the LORD. [9] "For *as* the heavens are higher than the earth, So are My ways higher than your ways And My thoughts than your thoughts.
> **Isaiah 55:6-9 (NASB)**

They are called Major Prophets because of the large amount of material they wrote not because their message was more important than any other prophet's. Key personalities are Isaiah, his two sons, Shearjashub and Maher-shalal-jash-baz. The purpose of the book of Isaiah was to call God's nation, the nation of Judah, back to faithfulness and to declare the coming Messiah "Immanuel". God calls and commissions His prophet to declare to Judah and Israel condemnation, conviction, and ultimately great hope.

---

[20]So he got up and came to his father. But while he was still a long way off, his father saw him and felt compassion *for him*, and ran and embraced him and kissed him. **Luke 15:20 (NASB)**

Ask: Does the idea of change scare you? Why/why not?

Point: Fear of the unknown and unfamiliar is the most common reason for not wanting to change, but fear is not a spirit of God and should never be used as the reason for making a decision

First Reading: 2 Timothy 1:6-7 (KJV)

First Reading
[6] Wherefore I put thee in remembrance that thou stir up the gift of God, which is in thee by the putting on of my hands. [7] For God hath not given us the spirit of fear; but of power, and of love, and of a sound mind.
2 Timothy 1:6-7 (KJV)

Re-read verse 7 from today's passage

Ask: What does "…return to the Lord…" mean?

Point: It means to repent.

Second Reading 2 Chronicles 7:14

Second Reading
[14] If my people, which are called by my name, shall humble themselves, and pray, and seek my face, and turn from their wicked ways; then will I hear from heaven, and will forgive their sin, and will heal their land.
2 Chronicles 7:14 (KJV)

Ask: Do not answer this question out loud but do you think you have anything to repent from?

Point: No one is perfect which means we all have something we need to be forgiven for.

Third Reading: 1 John 1:9

Ask: Is God a god of truth or lies?

Point: Fourth Reading: Numbers 23:19 (NASB following page)

State: Verse eight of today's passage clearly delineates Man's ways from God's ways. To this end study,

Third Reading
[7] but if we walk in the Light as He Himself is in the Light, we have fellowship with one another, and the blood of Jesus His Son cleanses us from all sin. [8] If we say that we have no sin, we are deceiving ourselves and the truth is not in us. [9] If we confess our sins, He is faithful and righteous to forgive us our sins and to cleanse us from all unrighteousness. [10] If we say that we have not sinned, we make Him a liar and His word is not in us.
1 John 1:7-10 (NASB)

[20]So he got up and came to his father. But while he was still a long way off, his father saw him and felt compassion *for him*, and ran and embraced him and kissed him. **Luke 15:20 (NASB)**

Christian conferencing or fellowship, and corporate worship help us learn more about His ways, which is how we communicate with the Holy Spirit to identify things God would like us to change in our lives.

Point: Fifth Reading: 2 Timothy 2:15 (NASB)

Ask: God then is truth and His word in the Bible is our guide but what about those things in which we are weak?

Point: Sixth Reading: 1 Corinthians 10:13 (NASB)

Seventh Reading: Phillipians 4:13 (NASB)

Closing Statement

In scripture, all roads lead to God, even Jesus for He said He is the only path to the Father. God's word is our tool, our guide, our manual for life. We need to be cautious as we move down this path though. As we study, read, and learn these are our lessons, our changes meant for our path. These things are not necessarily things for someone else's path. If what we learn is for others, God will ensure those "others" walk beside us as we learn, grow, and change. The watchwords here are Judgment and stumbling block. Hear what was written about these two very important, and interwoven concepts...

Fourth Reading
[19] "God is not a man, that He should lie, Nor a son of man, that He should repent; Has He said, and will He not do it? Or has He spoken, and will He not make it good?
Numbers 23:19 (NASB)

Fifth Reading
[15] Be diligent to present yourself approved to God as a workman who does not need to be ashamed, accurately handling the word of truth.
2 Timothy 2:15 (NASB)

Sixth Reading
[13] No temptation has overtaken you but such as is common to man; and God is faithful, who will not allow you to be tempted beyond what you are able, but with the temptation will provide the way of escape also, so that you will be able to endure it.
1 Corinthians 10:13 (NASB)

Seventh Reading
[13] I can do all things through Him who strengthens me.
Philippians 4:13 (NASB)

[11] For it is written, "AS I LIVE, SAYS THE LORD, EVERY KNEE SHALL BOW TO ME, AND EVERY TONGUE SHALL GIVE

---

[20]So he got up and came to his father. But while he was still a long way off, his father saw him and felt compassion *for him*, and ran and embraced him and kissed him. **Luke 15:20 (NASB)**

PRAISE TO GOD." [12] So then each one of us will give an account of himself to God. [13] Therefore let us not judge one another anymore, but rather determine this—not to put an obstacle or a stumbling block in a brother's way. [14] I know and am convinced in the Lord Jesus that nothing is unclean in itself; but to him who thinks anything to be unclean, to him it is unclean. [15] For if because of food your brother is hurt, you are no longer walking according to love. Do not destroy with your food him for whom Christ died. [16] Therefore do not let what is for you a good thing be spoken of as evil; [17] for the kingdom of God is not eating and drinking, but righteousness and peace and joy in the Holy Spirit. [18] For he who in this *way* serves Christ is acceptable to God and approved by men. [19] So then we pursue the things which make for peace and the building up of one another. [20] Do not tear down the work of God for the sake of food. All things indeed are clean, but they are evil for the man who eats and gives offense. [21] It is good not to eat meat or to drink wine, or *to do anything* by which your brother stumbles. [22] The faith which you have, have as your own conviction before God. Happy is he who does not condemn himself in what he approves. [23] But he who doubts is condemned if he eats, because *his eating is* not from faith; and whatever is not from faith is sin.

Romans 14:11-23 (NASB)
   Isaiah 45:23

---

[20]So he got up and came to his father. But while he was still a long way off, his father saw him and felt compassion *for him*, and ran and embraced him and kissed him. **Luke 15:20 (NASB)**

You Are Worthy
Sunday School Lesson 5
Maturing Your Christianity

"Spiritual maturity is not reached by the passing of years, but by the obedience to the will of God."

Oswald Chambers

Quote-Oswald Chambers

7/24/1874 to 11/15/1917 A Baptist, Chambers best known work a devotional titled *My Utmost for His Highest*, was actually compiled from notes taken by his widow, Gertrude "Biddy" Hobbs Chambers from his lectures and preaching. In October of 1917 Chambers came down with appendicitis but refused to go to the hospital siting the idea that the beds were needed by war-wounded from the Third Battle of Gaza. He died almost a month later and was buried in Cairo with full military honors.

> **Passage**
> [24] The Lord's bond-servant must not be quarrelsome, but be kind to all, able to teach, patient when wronged, [25] with gentleness correcting those who are in opposition, if perhaps God may grant them repentance leading to the knowledge of the truth, [26] and they may come to their senses *and escape* from the snare of the devil, having been held captive by him to do his will.
> **2 Timothy 2:24-26 (NASB)**

Passage-The book of 2nd Timothy is a Pastoral Epistle (letter from Paul to a church leader). The author is the Apostle Paul who wrote it approximately 67 A.D. and is probably his last letter. After Paul's release from his first imprisonment in Rome in AD 61 or 62, and after his final missionary journey (probably into Spain), he was again imprisoned under Emperor Nero c. 66-67. The key personalities are Paul, Timothy, Luke, Mark, and many others. Its purpose was to give direction to Timothy and urge him to visit one final time. From the somber nature of this letter, it is apparent that Paul knew that his work was done and that his life was nearly at an end (4:6-8).

---

[20]So he got up and came to his father. But while he was still a long way off, his father saw him and felt compassion *for him*, and ran and embraced him and kissed him. **Luke 15:20 (NASB)**

Ask: What does it mean to "be like Jesus?"
Point: For Christians it means trying to live our lives the way Jesus lived His life.

Ask: Do we do all things in our lives as Christ did in His life?
Point: The simple answer is no, we do not live all aspects of our lives, all actions in our lives, or all decisions made in our lives the way Jesus lived.

Ask: So, what should we do when we identify something in our own lives that does not conform to the way Jesus lived?
Point: The answer lies in the title of the fourth chapter of the book.

State: Each time we identify something in our lives that isn't aligned with how Jesus lived we have the choice that Joshua gave us, each and every time.
Point: First Reading: Joshua 24:15 (NASB)

> **First Reading**
> [15] "If it is disagreeable in your sight to serve the LORD, choose for yourselves today whom you will serve: whether the gods which your fathers served which were beyond the River, or the gods of the Amorites in whose land you are living; but as for me and my house, we will serve the LORD."
> **Joshua 24:15 (NASB)**

Ask: If God loves me just as I am, why change anything about myself?
Point: Second Reading: Luke 11:33 (NASB)

> **Second Reading**
> [33] "No one, after lighting a lamp, puts it away in a cellar nor under a basket, but on the lampstand, so that those who enter may see the light.
> **Luke 11:33 (NASB)**

State: Do you believe God has lit a light in you? Why or why not?
Point: If you claim the title of Christian, have made the choice, and accepted Jesus Christ as your savior, then God has lit a light in your life whether you are aware of it or not.

---

[20]So he got up and came to his father. But while he was still a long way off, his father saw him and felt compassion *for him*, and ran and embraced him and kissed him. **Luke 15:20 (NASB)**

Ask: Does the second reading answer the question of why we should change if God loves me as I am and has already lit a lamp with my life?

Point: Third Reading: Luke 11:34-36 (NASB)

Ask: When a mirror doesn't reflect the image in it clearly or completely or that reflection is either distorted or has some blemish what do we do with a mirror?

Point: We clean it so the reflection is a true representation of that which is reflected.

Fourth Reading: 2 Corinthians 3:18 (NASB)

Ask: Is Joshua's choice the end of a path or the beginning?

Point: It is both an end and a beginning. The end of the old self and the beginning of the new self, a new creation if you will.

Third Reading
34 "The eye is the lamp of your body; when your eye is clear, your whole body also is full of light; but when it is bad, your body also is full of darkness.
35 "Then watch out that the light in you is not darkness.
36 "If therefore your whole body is full of light, with no dark part in it, it will be wholly illumined, as when the lamp illumines you with its rays."
Luke 11:34-36 (NASB)

Fourth Reading
18 But we all, with unveiled face, beholding as in a mirror the glory of the Lord, are being transformed into the same image from glory to glory, just as from the Lord, the Spirit.
2 Corinthians 3:18 (NASB)

Fifth Reading: Ephesians 4:17-32 (NASB)
(The fifth reading is too long for a sidebar so it will be copied inline)

17 So this I say, and affirm together with the Lord, that you walk no longer just as the Gentiles also walk, in the futility of their mind,
18 being darkened in their understanding, excluded from the life of God because of the ignorance that is in them, because of the hardness of their heart; 19 and they, having become callous, have given themselves over to sensuality for the practice of every kind of impurity with greediness. 20 But you did not learn Christ in this way,
21 if indeed you have heard Him and have been taught in Him, just as truth is in Jesus, 22 that, in reference to your former manner of life, you lay aside the old self, which is being corrupted in accordance

20So he got up and came to his father. But while he was still a long way off, his father saw him and felt compassion *for him*, and ran and embraced him and kissed him. **Luke 15:20 (NASB)**

with the lusts of deceit, [23] and that you be renewed in the spirit of your mind, [24] and put on the new self, which in *the likeness of* God has been created in righteousness and holiness of the truth. [25] Therefore, laying aside falsehood, SPEAK TRUTH EACH ONE *of you* WITH HIS NEIGHBOR, for we are members of one another. [26] BE ANGRY, AND *yet* DO NOT SIN; do not let the sun go down on your anger, [27] and do not give the devil an opportunity. [28] He who steals must steal no longer; but rather he must labor, performing with his own hands what is good, so that he will have *something* to share with one who has need. [29] Let no unwholesome word proceed from your mouth, but only such *a word* as is good for edification according to the need *of the moment,* so that it will give grace to those who hear. [30] Do not grieve the Holy Spirit of God, by whom you were sealed for the day of redemption. [31] Let all bitterness and wrath and anger and clamor and slander be put away from you, along with all malice. [32] Be kind to one another, tender-hearted, forgiving each other, just as God in Christ also has forgiven you.
Ephesians 4:17-32 (NASB)
Zechariah 8:16
Psalm 4:3

Ask: What does "maturing your Christianity" mean?
Point: It means to heed the warning of Paul to Timothy about giving responsibility and position to new believers and is a warning to us as well who have a newly made decision or newly renewed decision but also to ensure we grow on God's path, not Man's path.

Sixth Reading: 1 Timothy 3:6 (NASB)

> **Sixth Reading**
> [6] *and* not a new convert, so that he will not become conceited and fall into the condemnation incurred by the devil.
> **1 Timothy 3:6 (NASB)**

Ask: If having just made the decision to follow Jesus is the milk, the immature Christian walk, what and or where is the mature Christian walk?
Point: Seventh Reading: Hebrews 5:13-14 (NASB)

> **Seventh Reading**
> [13] For everyone who partakes *only* of milk is not accustomed to the word of righteousness, for he is an infant. [14] But solid food is for the mature, who because of practice have their senses trained to discern good and evil.
> **Hebrews 5:13-14 (NASB)**

[20]So he got up and came to his father. But while he was still a long way off, his father saw him and felt compassion *for him*, and ran and embraced him and kissed him. **Luke 15:20 (NASB)**

Closing Statement

The immature Christian, the infant of Christianity is a person who is absolutely certain their position is the one right, true, and only way of God. No other position could possibly be in and of God if it disagrees with this toddler's viewpoint. However, the opposite is what is true. God is big enough that two people can read the same scripture and come away with opposite meanings, walk in opposite directions, and both still be on the path God has set for them. A path runs in two directions and has to destinations if someone starts in the middle. The passage for this lesson mentions how to correct "…those who are in opposition…" The King James uses different language, "…those who oppose themselves…" As infants in the ways of God we should be willing to acknowledge there are those who are wiser than we, know more than we, and understand more than we do. Because it is very prideful to assume we are the mature one, we should avoid arguments, being quarrelsome if you will. Let God and the Holy Spirit guide those who insist they are right because they might be. We should not be afraid to stand up and state what we believe, but not forceful or argumentative with those who have a different view. After all, we would not want to be labeled a "stumbling block", but we do want others to escape the "…snare of the devil…" and escape Satan's will. God has lit the candle of your life. Don't put that candle under the bushel basket of argument but rather set it on the lampstand of a living example, ever polishing the mirror to better reflect the perfect light of Christ through a life lived following His word of righteousness. This is maturing a walk with God, Jesus, and the Holy Spirit.

---

[20]So he got up and came to his father. But while he was still a long way off, his father saw him and felt compassion *for him*, and ran and embraced him and kissed him. **Luke 15:20 (NASB)**

[20]So he got up and came to his father. But while he was still a long way off, his father saw him and felt compassion *for him*, and ran and embraced him and kissed him. **Luke 15:20 (NASB)**

You Are Worthy
Sunday School Lesson 6

You Are Worthy

"You're imperfect and you're wired for struggle, but you are worthy of love and belonging."

Brene Brown

Quote- Casandra Brené Brown Ph.D. (11/18/65) is a research professor at the University of Houston and the author of five #1 New York Times bestsellers: *The Gifts of Imperfection, Daring Greatly, Rising Strong, Braving the Wilderness*, and *Dare to Lead*.

> [13] For You formed my inward parts; You wove me in my mother's womb.
> [14] I will give thanks to You, for I am fearfully and wonderfully made;
> Wonderful are Your works, And my soul knows it very well.
> **Psalm 139:13-14 (NASB)**

Passage- The genre of Psalms is Songs and Poetry of all kinds. It is written by multiple authors; David wrote 73, Asaph wrote 12, the sons of Korah wrote 9, Solomon wrote 3, Ethan, and Moses each wrote one (Ps. 90), and 51 of the Psalms are anonymous. They were written over the span of approximately 900 years (Beginning at the time of Moses 1440 B.C. and through the captivity in 586 B.C.).

The Psalms include praises of joy, laments, blessings, and thanksgivings. They are directed at God and they help us to express and communicate ourselves to Him. We read about the Psalmist's emotions from one extreme to another, from praising, delighting in and worshiping God with fervor, to repentance and crying out to Him in despair.

Psalms sits at the very center of the Bible. The major themes found in Psalms are Praise, God's Power, Forgiveness, Thankfulness and Trust. "My mouth will speak the praise of the LORD, and all flesh will bless His holy name forever and ever" (145:21).

---

[20]So he got up and came to his father. But while he was still a long way off, his father saw him and felt compassion *for him*, and ran and embraced him and kissed him. **Luke 15:20 (NASB)**

Ask: Why does God love you?
Point: This is an open-ended question designed to spark discussion on the subject

Ask: Do you believe God loves you?
Point: First Reading John 3:16 (NASB) John 3:16 confirms God loves everyone.

Ask: Do you believe God loves everyone else too and wants them walking in His ways…even those people you don't like very much?
Point: Second Reading John 3:17 (NASB) Jesus' job wasn't to condemn people but to save them

Ask: If God wants everyone following His ways, and Jesus didn't come to judge the world but save it, what implications does that have for us?
Point: Third Reading: Matthew 7:1-2 (NASB) We need to make sure we order our own lives in such a way as to reflect the values and beliefs we hold based on how scripture and the Holy Spirit inform us our lives are to be ordered.

Ask: Does "Do not judge…" mean not to have values, believe in right and wrong, and be willing to stand up for those?
Point: Fourth Reading: Matthew 5:17-20 (NASB)
(The fourth reading is too long for a sidebar so it will be copied inline)

> [17] "Do not think that I came to abolish the Law or the Prophets; I did not come to abolish but to fulfill. [18] "For truly I say to you, until heaven and earth pass away, not the smallest letter or stroke shall pass from the Law until all is accomplished. [19] "Whoever then annuls one of the least of these commandments, and teaches others *to do* the same, shall be called least in the kingdom of heaven; but whoever

---

First Reading
[16] "For God so loved the world, that He gave His only begotten Son, that whoever believes in Him shall not perish, but have eternal life.
John 3:16 (NASB)

Second Reading
[17] "For God did not send the Son into the world to judge the world, but that the world might be saved through Him.
John 3:17 (NASB)

Third Reading
[1] "Do not judge so that you will not be judged.
[2] "For in the way you judge, you will be judged; and by your standard of measure, it will be measured to you.
Matthew 7:1-2 (NASB)

---

[20]So he got up and came to his father. But while he was still a long way off, his father saw him and felt compassion *for him*, and ran and embraced him and kissed him. **Luke 15:20 (NASB)**

keeps and teaches *them,* he shall be called great in the kingdom of heaven. [20] "For I say to you that unless your righteousness surpasses *that* of the scribes and Pharisees, you will not enter the kingdom of heaven.
Matthew 5:17-20 (NASB)

Values, Standards, and morals are still there, still just as valid. Christians should have them and be a shining light on a lamppost as an example, but not trying to force those values onto anyone else's walk with God.

Ask: Is that a contradiction, "Do not judge…" and "…not the smallest letter or stroke shall pass from the law…"? How are Christians supposed to hold to God's standards as set forth in the law but not judge?
Point: Fifth Reading: Romans 14:12-13 (NASB) Each of us has our own path and will stand before God based on how we acted or didn't act, not based on how someone else did or didn't act.

> **Fifth Reading**
> [12] So then each one of us will give an account of himself to God.
> [13] Therefore let us not judge one another anymore, but rather determine this—not to put an obstacle or a stumbling block in a brother's way.
> **Romans 14:12-13 (NASB)**

> **Sixth Reading**
> [37] Then He said to His disciples, "The harvest is plentiful, but the workers are few.
> [38] "Therefore beseech the Lord of the harvest to send out workers into His harvest."
> **Matthew 9:37-38 (NASB)**

Ask: What makes me or you any judge of what God wants or doesn't want?
Point: Re-read today's passage. God has a specific path for each of us to walk with Him, Christ, and the Holy Spirit to serve His purpose in the world.

Ask: Why does God want me or you involved in His plan?
Point: Sixth Reading: Matthew 9:37-18 (NASB) Because there is a specific patch of the world only my or your gifts can reach and God would like to reach that portion of His harvest.

---

[20]So he got up and came to his father. But while he was still a long way off, his father saw him and felt compassion *for him*, and ran and embraced him and kissed him. **Luke 15:20 (NASB)**

Ask: How do we take in this harvest then?

Point: Seventh Reading: Mark 16:15 (NASB)

<u>**Seventh Reading**</u>
[15] And He said to them, "Go into all the world and preach the gospel to all creation. [16] "He who has believed and has been baptized shall be saved; but he who has disbelieved shall be condemned.
Mark 16:15-16 (NASB)

Closing Statement

In John 19:30 Jesus utters His final words on this world as a human being, "It is finished." This study is finished, but this is not the end. This is the beginning, a new beginning, a new creation has been done in you…if you choose. This new beginning, this new creation is a purpose from God, for God, with God. It isn't an easy path, but it is one that is shared by many others, a great cloud of witnesses if you will. These others are there to help you, comfort you, and guide you so long as you do the same for them. This is not a place nor a path of finger-pointing, accusations, or recriminations. This is a path of love, of kindness, and of assistance. It is a narrow path that leads to only one place, a place of holiness. Because the destination is holy, we who trod this path should try to make ourselves as presentable as possible based on who we are in a personal way. This path is not one of trying to remake others, but ourselves. In the process of becoming this new creation others see us, see what we have become, and want that for themselves. It becomes a path of example and mentoring when invited in. It becomes a path of talking with and listening to God for His intentions for our lives. It becomes a path of principle, courage, and bravery because God says, You Are Worthy.

[20]So he got up and came to his father. But while he was still a long way off, his father saw him and felt compassion *for him*, and ran and embraced him and kissed him. **Luke 15:20 (NASB)**

You Are Worthy
Sunday School Lesson 7
What Now?

"Catch on fire with enthusiasm and people will come from miles to watch you burn."

Charles Wesley

Quote: Charles Wesley (12/18/1707-3/29/1788) was the brother of John Wesley, the founder of what would become the United Methodist Church. Wesley was a prolific hymn writer penning over 6,500 hymns in his lifetime. One of his most well-known hymns is *Hark! The Herald Angels Sing.*

> **Passage**
> [15] And He said to them, "Go into all the world and preach the gospel to all creation. [16] "He who has believed and has been baptized shall be saved; but he who has disbelieved shall be condemned.
> **Mark 16:15-16 (NASB)**

Passage: The book of Mark is a Gospel that contains Narrative History, Sermons, Parables, and some Prophetic Oracles. This Gospel has somewhat of an emphasis on miracles (27 total) which is significantly more than any of the other Gospels. The keyword in Mark is "Immediately" which is used 34 times causing the reader to move from one account to the next rapidly. Mark is the shortest of the synoptic gospels and was written about 64 A.D. The key personalities of this book are Jesus Christ, His Twelve Disciples, Jewish religious leaders, Pilate, and John the Baptist.

The purpose of the Gospel of Mark is to show that the Lord Jesus is the Messiah, the Son of God who was sent to suffer and to serve to rescue and restore mankind.

State: You are worthy. God loves you. These are statements of value and usefulness, not righteousness and position. Let those feelings of inadequacy fall away, change, and become humility

---

[20]So he got up and came to his father. But while he was still a long way off, his father saw him and felt compassion *for him*, and ran and embraced him and kissed him. **Luke 15:20 (NASB)**

recognizing those aspects of your make up identified as weaknesses, God can use to His purpose if you let him.

First Reading: 2 Corinthians 12:7-9 (NASB)

Ask: Do you feel alone in this effort?
Point: God, Jesus, and the Holy Spirit walk with you, work with you, and are by your side.

Second Reading: Romans 8:31-39 (NASB)
(The Second reading is too long for a sidebar so it will be copied inline)

First Reading
[7] Because of the surpassing greatness of the revelations, for this reason, to keep me from exalting myself, there was given me a thorn in the flesh, a messenger of Satan to torment me—to keep me from exalting myself! [8] Concerning this I implored the Lord three times that it might leave me. [9] And He has said to me, "My grace is sufficient for you, for power is perfected in weakness." Most gladly, therefore, I will rather boast about my weaknesses, so that the power of Christ may dwell in me.
2 Corinthians 12:7-9 (NASB)

[31] What then shall we say to these things? If God *is* for us, who *is* against us? [32] He who did not spare His own Son, but delivered Him over for us all, how will He not also with Him freely give us all things? [33] Who will bring a charge against God's elect? God is the one who justifies; [34] who is the one who condemns? Christ Jesus is He who died, yes, rather who was raised, who is at the right hand of God, who also intercedes for us. [35] Who will separate us from the love of Christ? Will tribulation, or distress, or persecution, or famine, or nakedness, or peril, or sword? [36] Just as it is written, "FOR YOUR SAKE WE ARE BEING PUT TO DEATH ALL DAY LONG; WE WERE CONSIDERED AS SHEEP TO BE SLAUGHTERED." [37] But in all these things we overwhelmingly conquer through Him who loved us. [38] For I am convinced that neither death, nor life, nor angels, nor principalities, nor things present, nor things to come, nor powers, [39] nor height, nor depth, nor any other created thing, will be able to separate us from the love of God, which is in Christ Jesus our Lord.
Romans 8:31-39 (NASB)
Psalm 44:22

Ask: Does that mean we should do this without other people?

[20]So he got up and came to his father. But while he was still a long way off, his father saw him and felt compassion *for him*, and ran and embraced him and kissed him. **Luke 15:20 (NASB)**

Point: No, other people are not only valuable but are there to help and support us when we have difficulties.

Third Reading: Ecclesiastes 4:9-12 (NASB)

Ask: What should we do with this calling?
Point: Re-read the passage for today's lesson.

Ask: What directive does the passage from today's lesson give us as Christ's calling on Christian life?
Point: Verse fifteen has the answer; preach the Gospel.

Ask: When Jesus says "…preach the Gospel…" does He actually mean we are all to become pastors of a church and deliver messages to a congregation on Sunday?
Point: There are more ways to preach than just using words on Sunday from a pulpit.

Fourth Reading: Matthew 5:14-16 (NASB)

Ask: Scripture offers us a choice just like those in the Old testament.
Point: We can follow God, or we can follow Satan. This choice is presented to us as it was long ago to the people of Israel. We are those people today, and every day since. This choice remains with us, and not making a conscious choice, is a choice.

> **Third Reading**
> [9] Two are better than one because they have a good return for their labor. [10] For if either of them falls, the one will lift up his companion. But woe to the one who falls when there is not another to lift him up. [11] Furthermore, if two lie down together they keep warm, but how can one be warm *alone?* [12] And if one can overpower him who is alone, two can resist him. A cord of three *strands* is not quickly torn apart.
> **Ecclesiastes 4:9-12 (NASB)**

> **Fourth Reading**
> [14] "You are the light of the world. A city set on a hill cannot be hidden; [15] nor does *anyone* light a lamp and put it under a basket, but on the lampstand, and it gives light to all who are in the house. [16] "Let your light shine before men in such a way that they may see your good works, and glorify your Father who is in heaven.
> **Matthew 5:14-16 (NASB)**

---

[20]So he got up and came to his father. But while he was still a long way off, his father saw him and felt compassion *for him*, and ran and embraced him and kissed him. **Luke 15:20 (NASB)**

Fifth Reading: Joshua 24:15 (NASB)

Ask: Is there a third choice offered by Joshua? Is there any option other than a binary choice between God and Satan?

Point: Scripture does not give us a third alternative. We are either standing with God or we are Standing with Satan, which by definition is everything that is not God.

Sixth Reading: Matthew 12:30 (NASB)

Ask: Is there a deadline for all of this, for this decision, to start this preaching through living life?

Point: Yes. Now.

Seventh Reading: 2 Corinthians 6:1-2 (NASB)

Ask: Why does this decision have to be now?

Point: Because we are aware of it. We have become aware of the fork in the road. There is no way to continue down the path we have been on. We must go either left or right. Standing still, not wishing to choose between the two paths is itself a choice.

Ask: Which path is the right choice?

[20]So he got up and came to his father. But while he was still a long way off, his father saw him and felt compassion *for him*, and ran and embraced him and kissed him. **Luke 15:20 (NASB)**

Point: The path God has put in front of you where His ways, His word, and His ideas lead.

Eight Reading: Matthew 7:13-14 (NASB)

Ask: Why should we make this choice and move down this new path? Why not just stay where we are and continue to live as we have carrying the faith of Jesus in our hearts?

Point: Life, like time continues to move forward. You are moving down a path. There is no standing still. If you do not make a choice to follow Jesus, you will be forced down the path of least resistance, which is the wider of the two. Taking the narrow path through the narrow gate is done by force of will on a day to day basis, not passively going with the flow. Making the right choice here means following a guide, which we have in Jesus, the Christ.

Ninth Reading: John 15:6-11 (NASB)

Ask: What does it mean to bear fruit?

Point: It means to have results in our lives that are pleasing to God by following the example of Jesus.

Eight Reading

[13] "Enter through the narrow gate; for the gate is wide and the way is broad that leads to destruction, and there are many who enter through it. [14] "For the gate is small and the way is narrow that leads to life, and there are few who find it.
Matthew 7:13-14 (NASB)

Ninth Reading

[6] "If anyone does not abide in Me, he is thrown away as a branch and dries up; and they gather them, and cast them into the fire and they are burned. [7] "If you abide in Me, and My words abide in you, ask whatever you wish, and it will be done for you. [8] "My Father is glorified by this, that you bear much fruit, and *so* prove to be My disciples. [9] "Just as the Father has loved Me, I have also loved you; abide in My love. [10] "If you keep My commandments, you will abide in My love; just as I have kept My Father's commandments and abide in His love. [11] "These things I have spoken to you so that My joy may be in you, and *that* your joy may be made full.
John 15:6-11 (NASB)

[20]So he got up and came to his father. But while he was still a long way off, his father saw him and felt compassion *for him*, and ran and embraced him and kissed him. **Luke 15:20 (NASB)**

116

Ask: Where or how can we produce the most "fruit", the most results for Jesus in our lives?
Point: The point of this question is going to be different for each person based on the skills and abilities granted them from God and life-experiences.

Ask: What do Christians call these skills and abilities?
Point: Gifts.

Tenth Reading: Romans 12:4-13 (NASB)

Ask: Now what?

Closing Statement

Now what? What now is begin. Make the decision, pray to God, ask the Holy Spirit to guide you down the path of Jesus and go "preach the gospel" as only you can. We each have amazing individual gifts. Individual gifts. That means the skills and abilities differ from one person to another. This is by design to complement the efforts, one to the other not confound. We need to make sure we are helping others reach more people in Christ, not hindering them. But what happens if those we reach out to won't listen, or worse attack us for that message? Jesus Himself gave us instruction on how to deal with those who won't listen.

Tenth Reading
[4] For just as we have many members in one body and all the members do not have the same function,
[5] so we, who are many, are one body in Christ, and individually members one of another.
[6] Since we have gifts that differ according to the grace given to us, *each of us is to exercise them accordingly:* if prophecy, according to the proportion of his faith;
[7] if service, in his serving; or he who teaches, in his teaching;
[8] or he who exhorts, in his exhortation; he who gives, with liberality; he who leads, with diligence; he who shows mercy, with cheerfulness.
[9] *Let* love *be* without hypocrisy. Abhor what is evil; cling to what is good.
[10] *Be* devoted to one another in brotherly love; give preference to one another in honor;
[11] not lagging behind in diligence, fervent in spirit, serving the Lord;
[12] rejoicing in hope, persevering in tribulation, devoted to prayer,
[13] contributing to the needs of the saints, practicing hospitality.
Romans 12:4-13 (NASB)

---

[20] So he got up and came to his father. But while he was still a long way off, his father saw him and felt compassion *for him*, and ran and embraced him and kissed him. **Luke 15:20 (NASB)**

[11] "And whatever city or village you enter, inquire who is worthy in it, and stay at his house until you leave *that city.* [12] "As you enter the house, give it your greeting. [13] "If the house is worthy, give it your *blessing of* peace. But if it is not worthy, take back your *blessing of* peace. [14] "Whoever does not receive you, nor heed your words, as you go out of that house or that city, shake the dust off your feet. [15] "Truly I say to you, it will be more tolerable for *the* land of Sodom and Gomorrah in the day of judgment than for that city.
Matthew 10:11-15 (NASB)

Shake the dust off, meaning have nothing to do with them. They have chosen their fate and it is in God's hands now. If God should choose to send another and the Holy Spirit move their hearts to repentance or not, that is between God and those people. What now? Begin. Go. Produce fruit. Let no one be a stumbling block for another. Let brother and sister lift up one another in Jesus. Follow God. Eschew Man and his ways in favor of God and His ways. Be a light on a lamppost, an example. Let God use the areas where you are weak to demonstrate how He is strong. Go and preach the Gospel of Jesus Christ, not because you are righteous, holier than thou, or in some way better than other people. Go because God sees value in your life, has a purpose for your life, wants you involved in His purpose because He pronounced His creation good. You are part of that creation, which means, You Are Worthy!

---

[20]So he got up and came to his father. But while he was still a long way off, his father saw him and felt compassion *for him*, and ran and embraced him and kissed him. **Luke 15:20 (NASB)**

Made in the USA
Columbia, SC
21 February 2023

12702910R00065